# LIVING
# WITHOUT
# ENEMIES

Being Present in the Midst of Violence

## SAMUEL WELLS
## & MARCIA A. OWEN

Resources for Reconciliation

*series editors*

## EMMANUEL KATONGOLE & CHRIS RICE

IVP Books

An imprint of InterVarsity Press
Downers Grove, Illinois

InterVarsity Press
P.O. Box 1400, Downers Grove, IL 60515-1426
World Wide Web: www.ivpress.com
E-mail: email@ivpress.com

InterVarsity Press® is the book-publishing division of InterVarsity Christian Fellowship/USA®, a movement of students and faculty active on campus at hundreds of universities, colleges and schools of nursing in the United States of America, and a member movement of the International Fellowship of Evangelical Students. For information about local and regional activities, write Public Relations Dept., InterVarsity Christian Fellowship/USA, 6400 Schroeder Rd., P.O. Box 7895, Madison, WI 53707-7895, or visit the IVCF website at <www.intervarsity.org>.

Scripture quotations, unless otherwise noted, are from the New Revised Standard Version of the Bible, copyright 1989 by the Division of Christian Education of the National Council of the Churches of Christ in the USA. Used by permission. All rights reserved.

While all stories in this book are true, some names and identifying information in this book have been changed to protect the privacy of the individuals involved.

Design: Cindy Kiple
Images: Candle Light Vigil by Rick Beerhorst

ISBN 978-0-8308-3456-3

Printed in the United States of America ∞

**Library of Congress Cataloging-in-Publication Data**

Wells, Samuel, 1965-
    Living without enemies: being present in the midst of violence/
Samuel Wells and Marcia A. Owen.
        p. cm.—(Resources for reconciliation)
    Includes bibliographical references.
    ISBN 978-0-8308-3456-3 (pbk.: alk. paper)
    1. Nonviolence—Religious aspects—Christianity. 2. Love—Religious
aspects—Christianity. 3. Church work. 4. Violence—North
Carolina—Durham. 5. Violence—North Carolina—Durham—Prevention
I. Owen, Marcia A., 1955- II. Title.
    BT736.6.W45 2011
    261.8'3—dc22

2011006817

| P | 19 | 18 | 17 | 16 | 15 | 14 | 13 | 12 | 11 | 10 | 9 | 8 | 7 | 6 | 5 | 4 | 3 | 2 | 1 |
|---|----|----|----|----|----|----|----|----|----|----|---|---|---|---|---|---|---|---|---|
| Y | 27 | 26 | 25 | 24 | 23 | 22 | 21 | 20 | 19 | 18 | 17 | 16 | 15 | 14 | 13 | 12 | 11 | | | |

*For Tony Williams*

# Contents

# Series Preface

*The Resources for Reconciliation Book Series*

*A* partnership between InterVarsity Press and the Center for Reconciliation at Duke Divinity School, Resources for Reconciliation books address what it means to pursue hope in areas of brokenness, including the family, the city, the poor, the disabled, Christianity and Islam, racial and ethnic divisions, violent conflicts and the environment. The series seeks to offer a fresh and distinctive vision for reconciliation as God's mission and a journey toward God's new creation in Christ. Each book is authored by two leading voices, one in the field of practice or grassroots experience, the other from the academy. Each book is grounded in the biblical story, engages stories and places of pain and hope, and seeks to help readers to live faithfully—a rich mix of theology, context and practice.

This book series was born out of the mission of the Duke Divinity School Center for Reconciliation: *Advancing God's mission of reconciliation in a divided world by cultivating new leaders, communicating wisdom and hope, and connecting in outreach to strengthen leadership.* A divided world needs people with the vision, spiritual maturity and daily skills integral to the journey of reconciliation. The church needs fresh resources—a mix of biblical vision, social skills of social and historical analysis, and practical gifts of spirituality and social leadership—in order to pursue reconciliation in real places, from congregations to communities.

The ministry of reconciliation is not reserved for experts. It is the core of God's mission and an everyday call of the Christian life. These books are written to equip and stimulate God's people to be more faithful ambassadors of reconciliation in a fractured world.

For more information, email the Duke Divinity School Center for Reconciliation at reconciliation@div.duke.edu, or visit our website: <http://divinity.duke.edu/initiatives-centers/center -reconciliation>.

*Emmanuel Katongole*
*Chris Rice*
Center codirectors and series editors

# Acknowledgments

*M*any people stand in the background of this project, and two stand in the foreground. Those in the background include Mel Williams and Leslie Dunbar, who cofounded the Religious Coalition for a Nonviolent Durham; David Winer, former executive director of Durham Congregations In Action, who first led the vigils; Rodney and Yolanda Ellis and the members of The Wave, a start-up church in Durham; Anna Lee Mosley, Diane Jones, Ruthy Jones, Bernic Page, Nellie Jones, Gudrun Parmer, Brenda James, Kacey Reynolds, Joanie Ross, Leah Wilson-Hartgrove, Linda Karolak, Effie Steele, Maryann Crea, Betty Grant, Mina Hampton, Judi Vos, Ethel Simonetti and all the peacemakers whose leadership has sustained the coalition; and all who have attended luncheons, served as directors, offered prayers, joined vigils and been part of re-entry faith teams over the years.

Chris Rice, Emmanuel Katongole and Jonathan Wilson-

Hartgrove initiated this book by putting together the series and inviting us to be part of it. Several friends have reviewed the manuscript and made helpful suggestions, notably John Kiess, Mack Dennis and Mary Ellen Ashcroft. Rebekah Eklund did a marvelous, patient, expert and irreplaceable job of transcribing interviews, pulling together source material, reviewing and correcting the manuscript, suggesting alterations and improving the book in countless ways.

A great many people have shared their experiences of what it is like to be a family member of a homicide victim. Among them we are especially grateful to Brenda James for giving permission to quote her words. Another cloud of witnesses related their experience of coming out of prison and joining a re-entry faith team. Among them we want to thank Corey Wise, who partners with Durham Friends Meeting; Cubbi Edwards, who partners with Duke Chapel; Travis Sellers, who partners with Sanctuary United Methodist Church, Lakewood, Durham; and Dorsey Williams, who partners with Trinity United Methodist Church, Durham. They offered the reflections that introduce each chapter of this book. Alongside those reflections are further testimonies from representatives among those involved in local congregations who have joined re-entry faith teams as members: Ron Landfried, Ira Mueller and Michael Somich. While all the stories in this book are true, some names and identifying details have been changed to protect the privacy of those involved.

In the foreground stands Abby Kocher, whose conversations with us made this book possible, whose witness is an embodiment of and testimony to the commitments represented by this book and who, alongside many colleagues, did so much to make the coalition a part of the life of Duke Chapel and Duke Chapel a part of the life of the coalition. And finally there lies Tony Williams, whose story is told in detail in chapter six and to whom, in humble witness and thanks, this book is dedicated.

*Samuel Wells and Marcia A. Owen*

# Introduction

*W*e met in the summer of 2005. Sam had just moved from England to Durham, North Carolina, to become the dean of Duke University Chapel. He set about finding out what local churches and student groups were up to. He wanted to know where they believed Christ was most frequently in the habit of showing up, and he wanted to learn how to "hang out" (a new expression to him) in those places.

Sam was intrigued to hear that there was to be a prayer vigil on a street on the other side of town to commemorate the life of a young man who had been murdered on that same spot a few weeks before. This sounded like just the kind of place where Sam might expect Christ to show up, so he decided to go along. At the vigil he discovered a dozen people who had gathered in the sweltering heat of an August evening to say prayers, hold mementos, listen to relatives of the victim, keep silence and show tenderness and grace to one another.

Sam felt this was one of the most beautiful things he'd ever seen. It expressed almost everything he believed about ministry and almost everything he believed about God. He had never felt that ministry—or God—was about making things happy. He'd long felt that the heart of ministry—and the heart of God—is about making things beautiful, even when they can't be happy. But in fifteen years of ministry, he'd never seen anything that embodied that conviction quite as well as this.

And there in this small crowd, saying little but hugging much, was Marcia, who had coordinated the vigil. Sam and Marcia embraced before they ever spoke. They met God in one another before they knew one another's names. They have continued to meet God in one another and in the people they have brought into one another's lives in the six years since that first meeting. This book is about that meeting, those people and that God.

Marcia had attended many vigils through her longstanding involvement with the Religious Coalition for a Nonviolent Durham. On this occasion, once again, the vigil had humbled and saddened her beyond words and reason. Those gathered were mourning a fifteen-year-old boy who'd been shot, allegedly by another teenager. There was no appearance of power or influence anywhere—no building, rules of worship, fame, money, scholarship or institution at all. Upon reflection (now), Marcia admits her surprise in meeting Sam that afternoon in such an unregarded place, a person with a prestigious title from an elite institution. She thought she needed to explain to him what was happening. She remembers finding the words to say, "The only response to our immeasurable loss is God's immeasurable love."

He nodded and smiled. There was mostly silence and touch. And there followed only a few words.

\* \* \*

This is a book about violence, especially gun violence in one city. But it has applications well beyond that issue and well beyond that city. It is a book about overcoming powerlessness and fear. It is written for any who feel drawn to care about issues that plague our lives and societies, and to care about the people at the center of them, but who are unsure how to engage with such issues and are paralyzed with fear at the prospect of meeting those most closely involved in them. It's about learning to love the stranger and making first steps in forming relationships across social boundaries. It's for those who are discovering that poverty is a mask we put on a person to cover up his or her real wealth and that wealth is a disguise we put on a person to hide his or her profound poverty. In the end, this book aspires to a renewal of the Christian vision not just of ministry but also of God.

This book blends the experience and reflection of its two authors. In chapter one, Sam draws on his many years living and working in socially disadvantaged neighborhoods and surveys four overlapping but distinct styles of engagement. Chapter two incorporates Marcia's journey and shows how her understanding of the issue of gun violence changed, grew and was eventually transformed in ways that illustrate and illuminate these different styles of engagement.

In the following three chapters, Sam offers a shape and narrative that brings together Marcia's rich and challenging experiences of meeting and sharing God through her work as part-time director of the Religious Coalition for a Nonviolent Durham, and highlights our shared convictions. The book concludes with an event that brought our ministries together and crystallized everything we each believe about reconciliation. Finally, Marcia offers ten gleanings distilled from her years in this ministry.

# I

# Nazareth

*I think about all the young people I talk to about stopping the drugs and the violence. My life can give them hope.*

Dorsey, re-entry faith team partner[1]

*I've been in Durham seventeen years now. And in that time, more than five hundred people have died by homicide. And how many people have been shot but survived? Unfortunately, we either don't keep those statistics or we don't make those numbers public. Probably because the powers that be think we would be shocked by the total.*

Ron, re-entry faith team member

After her second son was born, Marcia was part of an AIDS care team at her local United Methodist church. She had joined the team because so many of her friends and acquaintances had died of or become infected with HIV. But they were all in New York City, and she was now in Durham, North Carolina. And she felt called to respond to the reality of AIDS where she was. The ministry coordinator wanted the team to care for a mother and two children. One of the things the team was going to need to do was to transport the children to the hospital, because they would often get dangerous fevers in the middle of the night. An ambulance wasn't necessary—they just needed a ride. But when the location of their home was mentioned to the team, everybody said, in essence, "That's too dangerous. I really couldn't do that."

When she heard this, Marcia felt an explosion of consciousness inside her. Feeling sympathy arising in her from being a mother herself, she remembers saying out loud, "But there are *children* there." It dawned on her that this was a neighborhood within her own hometown that was so violent that some people would never enter it. To Marcia, this suddenly seemed monstrously unjust. She kept thinking, "God have mercy on us. There are *children* living in this neighborhood."

It became vividly apparent to Marcia that *all* of Durham was her community, not just her own neighborhood. There was no place that was "outside" her community. And that she would love beyond fear. She could not live comfortably with the knowledge that there were neighborhoods where children were living in danger from gun violence. She didn't blame or judge the people who said, "I can't go there." Because they were right. It *was* dangerous. When somebody discharges a weapon, it puts everybody in the vicinity at risk. You don't know what or whom that bullet is going to hit. And *children* were there. So Marcia made an agreement with the AIDS care ministry that she would just be on her own in that neighborhood with their supervision and support.

The ministry coordinator introduced her to the mother and her two children, who were all HIV-positive. The children's ages were on either side of Marcia's son's age. The mother introduced Marcia to the other young mothers in the neighborhood. The place was brimming with children. A beautiful young woman asked, "Would you walk down and see my house?" And she took Marcia upstairs and pointed to her baby's crib, and there, an inch or two above the railing, were bullet holes. The mother said, "This happened last night."

Other mothers told Marcia they put their children to bed in the bathtub, because it's the safest place for them, because of drive-by shootings. They heard gunshots day and night. The bathtub was the one place they felt was safe. (Over the years Marcia has had friends call her from inside their furnace room, because they thought that would be the safest place to hide while all the bullets were flying.) These conversations confirmed the concerns of the people in Marcia's AIDS care team at church, and it confirmed to Marcia that this was not what God wanted for this community—that this was not the kingdom.

"We put our children to bed in the bathtub, because it's the safest place for them." These words haunted Marcia. How could she respond to these words? She quickly realized this wasn't just a question for her. In trying to answer this question, Marcia has made many discoveries. Those discoveries are what this book is about.

This is where those discoveries began: Something is wrong. People are suffering. Something can, should, must be done about it. But what? Who should do it? How, when and where should it be done? And will it do any good? These are the questions that cause paralysis, despair and cynicism. Not wanting to do the wrong thing in the wrong place at the wrong time in the wrong way for the wrong reasons holds many—perhaps most—people back from doing anything at all. Especially about an issue like gun violence.

And so in a city like Durham, North Carolina, the blood of twenty-five to thirty people a year continues to cry from the ground. Eighty percent of those who are murdered are victims of gunshot wounds. In the United States as a whole, eighty-five people die every day from gun violence; nine of these are children. Every year, about thirty thousand Americans, including three thousand children, die the same way. Children in the United States are sixteen times more likely to be killed with a gun than children in twenty-five other industrialized countries combined.[2] These are the cries Marcia heard; these are the reasons she knew her struggle was not just a personal, local one.

This is the story of a particular response to the particular tragedy of gun violence. But its insights are intended to apply to many challenging questions in many demanding contexts. There are many issues that evoke fear and bewilderment. There are many people who enjoy or endure circumstances very different from or challenging to their own. The aim of this chapter is to offer a vocabulary for thinking about good and less good ways of engaging with such people and such issues.

## Four Models of Engagement

Most congregations have a willing and generous member who starts every conversation by asking, "How can I help?" Many of us would like to think of ourselves as such a person. And yet sometimes it's not a bad idea to wait and listen for a while before assuming you're the right person, in the right place, at the right time to be genuinely helpful. How do you know? Here is a scenario that illustrates ways to answer that question.

Imagine you are in the parking lot of a grocery store, and you see a person leaving the store, struggling to carry a huge pile of shopping bags. Let's leave aside the possibility that you simply say, "It's not my problem," thus successfully banishing the person's plight from your imagination and conscience. Let's assume instead that your hands are empty and your heart is willing. What might you do? Let's look at four options.

Option one is to say, "Here, let me get those for you." You approach the beleaguered grocery shopper and offer to carry the bags back to his or her car. This is, on the face of it, a simple task that won't take much time. There is every chance it will end with a heartfelt "Thank you!" and a reciprocal "You're welcome. Have a great day." This is what might be called the conventional model of engagement. It may be called *working for*. You are *working for* the person by carrying the bags to the car.

Option two is to say, "I can see that's a lot of bags for anyone to carry. How about if you let me carry the awkwardly shaped ones, since I'm a bit taller than you, and you carry the more compact ones. That way you'll get to your car without anything falling out of the bags, or the bags collapsing—or you collapsing." Here, a more complex relationship is emerging. You are expressing a little more respect by acknowledging that the person exiting the grocery store may wish to carry his or her own bags. You are articulating a sense that each person—you and the overburdened shopper—has something to contribute to the task of getting to the car and that you can achieve something together that neither of you could achieve separately. This approach may be called *working with*. You are *working with* the person by entering a shared project in which you harness different analyses and skills through which the bags may best reach the car.

Option three is to say, "That looks like a lot of hard work. I wonder if a lot of your life feels like carrying a heavy load like that. May I walk alongside you as you carry your bags? I can carry some if you like, but I'm not assuming you're looking for someone to take your heavy load away. I'm guessing instead you're looking for someone to be alongside you in your struggles and not leave you isolated and alone." This is a conversation that's open to misinterpretation. It could be seen as a withholding of assistance, if the person is genuinely looking for nothing less or more than one-time practical help. On the other hand, it could be seen as a communication of respect and an act of humility that doesn't offer instant solutions, even to a relatively simple difficulty. This approach may be called *being with*. You are *being with* the person by offering wholehearted physical presence, but you are going out of your way to emphasize that the agency in the situation is wholly theirs, not something you can or perhaps should seek to take away from them, even if it might seem to make their circumstances more comfortable. You may seldom if ever actually get to articulate all these sentiments in words as precise as the ones above, but you will become increasingly adept at expressing them in nonverbal ways.

Option four is to say, "I'm really concerned and passionate on behalf of brothers and sisters who are carrying heavy loads. However, I can't go and help or stand alongside that person right now. I'm a little frightened, I'm a little shy, and I don't really know how to begin a relationship with a stranger in a parking lot. I don't want my actions to be misinterpreted, and I have some other things elsewhere I need to be doing. But I strongly believe that it's God's will for us to bear one another's burdens, and I want my life to be so oriented that I see the struggles of others and don't avert my gaze." This internal dialogue could be a form of self-deception, but it may be perfectly genuine. It assumes the person is trying hard to avoid saying, "Not my problem." This may be called *being for*. It has things in common with *being with*, because it does not assume it is possible, or even appropriate, always to bring a solution to the problems of others. And it has aspects in common with *working for*, in that those others are not directly brought into the deliberation about what is the best course of action.

Within the limitations of a spontaneous, interpersonal example within a short time frame, this outline offers in broad terms the chief characteristics of four approaches to engagement: *working for, working with, being with* and *being for.*

It is important to emphasize that these are not watertight categories, but broad tendencies: it is perfectly possible for an approach to overlap more than one of these models.[3] For example, each approach has been an important component of Marcia's encounter with the problem of gun violence in the city of Durham, as we will see in the next chapter. There also is an appropriate time and place for each one of these categories. The point of setting them out so explicitly is to observe how so much Christian social engagement is oriented to the default setting of *working for*, and not only to severely question that orientation but also to show how *working with* and especially *being with* may be more appropriate and more faithful forms of witness.

Now that we've sketched out the four approaches, we want to draw them into a wider frame of reference, so it becomes clear that each one represents a significant tendency in coming to terms with the tensions that surround social engagement.

## ILLUSTRATING THE FOUR APPROACHES

*Working for.* This is the conventional model of engagement across class and race boundaries. One person has a need, while the other person has skills, availability and willingness to help. This latter person conventionally spends a lot of time working those skills up to a very high standard and consequently makes those skills available in specific circumstances under strict rules.

This is what is known as being a professional. It is what most medical professions are about; it is what the legal profession is about; it is what dentistry is about. Physicians, attorneys and dentists do *for* us what we cannot do for ourselves.

It is hard to overestimate the hold this conventional model has on our imaginations. Pretty much the whole of a university's professional school structure—medicine, law, nursing, engineering, environment studies—runs on this model. Almost every undergraduate who goes to college wanting to make the world a better place assumes that this is the way it is done: you become very good at what you do, and you spend the rest of your life doing it *for* people.

There are three illustrations of this *working for* model as it applies to engaging issues of social inequality and dislocation. One is to concentrate on acquiring and discharging executive and legisla tive power. The places of controversy in a city tend to be the city council and the school boards. Those who seek to keep authority in the hands of people of property and wealth seek to consolidate influence by taking up seats on such bodies. Those who seek to represent less dominant voices or perspectives may also seek seats on these bodies. The motives and intentions of these diverse parties may be the very best, or they may not. The point is that in a representative democracy, even the most well-intentioned representatives assume their role is to speak for underrepresented groups and individuals. It somehow seems impossible or inefficient or unnecessary to create circumstances in which such people can speak for themselves. In the legal justice system, the emphasis is precisely to avoid people needing to speak up for themselves.

Another illustration of *working for* is found in philanthropy. There is a familiar trajectory in our culture by which the entrepreneur strikes out a path in business, makes a modest fortune in doing so and then in midlife senses it's time to "give something back." "Giving back" requires a different set of skills from acquiring wealth. The entrepreneur's instinct tends to be to provide visible infrastructure—in the way of signature buildings and landscapes—that epitomizes a new dawn in the life of disadvantaged people. More difficult can be persuading such disadvantaged people that these new buildings and landscapes are the fulfillment of their dreams.

A third illustration is found in international relief and development. This is perhaps the most evident area where *working for* assumptions can be seen in sharp relief. It is easy to assume in a land of many waterborne diseases that what is most needed is a well. And an engineer from a highly developed economy may be able to organize the building of a well quickly and efficiently. From there it's a short step to assuming that the state or country needs not just new wells but a new education system, so people understand how to use wells and other forms of technology. Such logic takes some to the point of assuming that the nation needs not just new wells and a new education system but also a new government. Thus we arrive at the notion of regime change, an extreme *working for* solution. It is not difficult to draw analogies between this style of international development and local forms of engagement.

**Working with.** Turning to *working with* again, three examples may illustrate the assumptions of such an approach. Each of the examples sets aside the assumption that the solution (and, in fact, the diagnosis) comes from the "expert." Each instead seeks to empower a group of people to discover their own solutions based on their own diagnoses.

One dynamic organization in Durham is Triangle Residential Options for Substance Abusers (TROSA). Those with a determination to overcome varying forms of addiction take up residency on the TROSA campus for about two years. The organization runs a number of businesses, including household moving, yard work and picture framing, in which the residents may participate while they make steps toward their own rehabilitation. TROSA is a combined enterprise among the residents, a substantial staff (more than half of whom are former residents) and professional experts in various fields, such as psychiatry.

Another vibrant circle in Durham is a combination of congregations, associations and neighborhoods appropriately known as Durham CAN (Durham Congregations, Associations, Neighborhoods). It is a grassroots movement dedicated to social change. It develops people's sense of their own power by taking on collective action campaigns directed at achievable, quantifiable goals, such as securing fair hiring and probationary practices at a local hospital. The sense of empowerment gained through securing social victories is as important as the changes achieved.

A more famous international example of *working with* is Grameen Bank, for whose foundation and development Muhammad Yunus won the 2006 Nobel Peace Prize. Grameen Bank helps impoverished Bangladeshi women escape from the clutches of abject poverty by providing them with low-interest, micro-credit loans. When provided with the loans, the women form a solidarity group that takes and adheres to sixteen decisions that inculcate discipline, unity, courage and hard work. Here again economic expertise is present, but occupies one seat at the table along with many others. A roundtable of energies brings about social change, and people know they have made the decisive moves themselves.

*Being with.* The approach of *being with* is less given to programs and movements, and is more to be found in piecemeal initiatives and small-scale relationships. This is because *being with* is not fundamentally about finding solutions, but about companionship amid struggle and distress. Sometimes the obsession with finding solutions can get in the way of forming profound relationships of mutual understanding, and sometimes those relationships are more significant than solutions. Nonetheless, some more widely known examples of *being with* may be offered as illustrations.

Jean Vanier's work with L'Arche is a prominent form of *being with*. L'Arche communities are family-like homes where people with and without disabilities share their lives together, giving witness to the reality that persons with disabilities possess inherent qualities of welcome, wonderment, spirituality and friendship. Members of L'Arche believe that these qualities, expressed through vulnerability and simplicity, actually make those with a disability the real teachers about what is most important in life: to love and to be loved.

The hospice movement is a comparatively recent development

within the medical world that seeks humane ways to enhance the experience and process of dying. Most importantly, it heightens awareness of the importance of patients as unique human beings with individual needs and rights, and as deserving of respect. The physician Cicely Saunders was inspired in the 1960s by a terminally ill patient who, at the end of life, requested words of comfort and acts of kindness and friendship. Saunders came to believe and to teach, "We do not have to cure to heal."

The New Monasticism movement, associated with figures such as Shane Claiborne in Philadelphia, has brought to the attention of evangelical Christians the significance of setting up home in poorer urban neighborhoods. In a similar way the Catholic Worker movement, inspired by Dorothy Day in 1933, has emphasized living with materially disadvantaged people and performing works of mercy, rather than simply seeking legislative change. Catholic Workers adopt lives of voluntary poverty so as to be free for direct, personal involvement. They seek not so much to dispense charity as to share in the lives of others.[4] Such initiatives are more appropriate to the extent that they come about at the invitation of residents of such neighborhoods, rather than simply at the decision of those who feel a call to such ventures.

*Being for.* It is easy to fall into seeing *being for* as simply a poor relation to the other three approaches. In some ways it carries the negative associations of *being with* (not producing any concrete change) with the negative connotations of *working for* (not actually asking the disadvantaged or suffering person what she or he sees as the problem and the way forward). These are real dangers. But these criticisms can also be unfair, as the following three examples illustrate.

Many university academics could be described as fulfilling a *being for* approach. Their research may not specifically address issues of race and class, and their students may not in every instance or even in many cases subsequently work or live in close relation to the issues. But still these professors may feel that their lives are lived for the sake of the disadvantaged, and many of their educational, consumer and other domestic choices and commitments may reflect such an ethos.

The historic tradition of monasticism, particularly the Benedictine tradition with its vow of stability and its daily round of prayer, may be taken as typical of the quest to be poor in spirit and to adopt a lifestyle that points to God's care for the poor. Such prayer is committed to *being with* God, with the people on your heart—even if you're not tangibly interacting with disadvantaged people.

Finally, many who have been wholly and unambiguously committed to some version of *working for*, *working with* or *being with* may find in retirement, and specifically in their advanced years, that they can regard *being for* as a fulfillment of their commitments in a way that asks less of their waning physical and perhaps mental and emotional strength.

## EXPLORING THE FOUR APPROACHES

We've looked at some institutional examples of these four approaches. What do they look like when translated into interpersonal terms?

**Working for.** Let's start once again with *working for*. It is immensely satisfying to be able to do *for* someone exactly what he or she needs done, whether it's fixing a child's toy or showing a novice how to find a website on a computer. We can see an end result, and it affirms us as people of skill and ability. In many cases it makes the recipient's life materially better—and in the work of a physician or firefighter, it may even make the difference between life and death.

So why do professional people so often find that their clients don't say thank you? The reason is that *working for* makes the expert feel good and important and useful, but it does not necessarily leave the recipient feeling that great. The *working for* model sets in stone a relationship in which one person is a benefactor and the other is a person in need. It is humiliating if many or most of your relationships are ones in which you need someone to do things *for* you. The *working for* model perpetuates relationships of inequality.

Worse still, it is possible to be the recipient of a person's help and still find the benefactor remains a stranger to you. The whole point of the professional infrastructure of divided offices, administrative assistants, appointment times and special uniforms is to remind all parties that this is not a friendship with expectations of compassion and tenderness. Instead it is the provision of a service, with no strings attached outside and beyond that service. The *working for* model dominates contemporary notions of welfare, but it leaves the rich and the poor pretty much where they started off, and it keeps them strangers to one another.

Think back for a moment to the person emerging from the

grocery store with too many shopping bags to carry to the car. It's natural to say, "Here, let me get those *for* you," and thus initiate a *working for* relationship. But will the person always say, "Thanks so much"? No, she or he will not, for one of two reasons. The first is that the person may feel patronized—particularly if there is a sensitive dynamic of gender, age or disability. For some people, it is better to struggle on alone than get on the receiving end of any kind of *working for* relationship that simply reinforces their lowly social standing. Some may interpret this as pride, but often it is more about preserving self-respect. The other reason the person might say no is because he or she thinks you might run off with the groceries. So these two factors, *empowerment* and *trust*, tend to be missing in *working for* relationships. The issue of empowerment is taken up in the approach of *working with*, and the issue of trust is taken up in *being with*.

**Working with.** *Working with* disadvantaged people means recognizing that social and economic disadvantage is not just about lacking income, but also about being excluded from positions of power. Disadvantaged people themselves must define what their needs are and then be supported in the action they decide to take to change things. This involves entering into a reciprocal *relationship* with disadvantaged people. It means surrendering some of your own autonomy and sense of power in being able to identify what needs to be done and taking steps to make a difference. It means offering what you have and are for another person's use.[5] It means never doing something *for* people that they could properly do for themselves.

*Working with* means bringing different skills and experience together around a common goal. It can create a wonderful sense of partnership—if the agenda is being set by the person in need rather than the person trying to help. Instead of a professional relationship, in which the person in need sees the benefactor entirely on the benefactor's terms and in a relationship dictated by the benefactor's priorities, the *working with* model depicts a roundtable where each person present has a different but equally valuable portfolio of experience, skills, interests, networks and commitments.

The *working with* model also recognizes that the journey is as important as the destination. When you go on a long journey, you can spend a great deal of time with traveling companions and experience a number of unexpected adventures before reaching the destination. When you look back on the expedition, you may find yourself dwelling as much or more on the companions and the adventures as you do on the destination itself and what took place there. This is how medieval quests and pilgrimages worked: the conversations and adventures people had on the way mattered as much and shaped character as significantly as the place they were walking toward. The same is true of *working with*. *Working with* is not so much about giving people better material conditions and facilities; it is about making *new people*, inspired and empowered and finding new skills and confidence through being given responsibility and access to conversations that have wider influence.

To take a familiar example, there are a number of institutions in any major American city where a homeless person can find an evening meal. The conventional model, *working for*, suggests that what the homeless person needs is an evening meal. But simply providing an evening meal reinforces the people in their poverty and leaves them hungry again tomorrow. So the familiar distinction between the "deserving" and "undeserving" poor separates the person who needs help up through a tough time from the person who will keep coming back for meals however often they're available. The logic often goes on to assume that the only way to help the "undeserving" poor is to punish them until they learn to fend for themselves.

Advocates of the empowerment model, *working with*, are not content until the homeless person not only sets the menu but also does the cooking. In this view, community kitchens exist not to produce *meals* but to empower *people*, and the post of director of the kitchen should change every few years as a new homeless person comes through the ranks to take over the reins. Before long the question of why people continue to go hungry in the city should bring all kinds of people—business leaders, city managers and welfare advisers—around the table with homeless people to empower such people to resolve their own problems at the table of power. *Working with* is essentially about realizing that a social problem is everyone's problem. It is about *everyone* getting to feel satisfaction in resolving that problem, which in the conventional model only the professional person gets.[6]

**Being with.** *Being with* addresses the issue of trust we left unresolved when we were wondering whether we could take those shopping bags back to the overburdened person's car. *Being with* disadvantaged people means experiencing *in your own life* something of what it is to be disempowered and oppressed. It means setting aside your plans and strategies for change and simply *feel-ing with* disadvantaged people the pain of their situation. It in-volves seeing the implications poverty has for people's sense of themselves and their connections with one another—not only their material well-being. It dispels an easy view of poverty as romantic and of disadvantaged people as simple and virtuous. It means seeing tensions and contradictions within and between disadvantaged people and more advantaged people, and recog-nizing through this that *all* of us are part of the problem. Poverty is not just *out there*, but *within us*, whoever we are.[7]

The *working with* model already added an extra dimension to approaching complicated problems like poverty. *Being with* goes yet a step further. It means experiencing *in your own body* some of the fragility of relationships, self-esteem and general well-being that are at the heart of poverty. It means having the patience not to search around for the light switch, but to sit side by side for a time in the shadows. Job's comforters are much maligned, but it is often forgotten that when they came to Job and saw the depth of his suffering, "they sat with him on the ground seven days and seven nights, and no one spoke a word to him, for they saw that his suffering was very great" (Job 2:13).

*Being with* is incomprehensible to an imagination that has been entirely shaped by the conventional *working for* model. After all, how can you hope to solve anyone's problems if you divest your-self not only of the safety of professional boundaries but of the skills that go with them? You have to come to see that poverty is not fundamentally a problem to be solved. The *working for* model—and some versions of the *working with* model—tends to turn everything into a problem ripe for solving. But some things aren't problems, and some problems cannot simply be fixed.

Just imagine *working for* and *working with* have done their stuff and achieved all they set out to do. What then, when there is no world to fix? We get to "hang out." In other words, we *enjoy* one another. We enjoy the actions and habits of life because they make us realize how good it is to be alive, how good it is to be a person among others, how good it is to be a person in the created world, how good it is to be a child of God. The *being with* approach says, "Let's not leave those discoveries till after all the solving and fixing is done and we're feeling bored. Let's make those discoveries now."

To say to someone, "I want to be with you," is to say, "When I'm with you I feel in touch with myself, in touch with what it means to be a human being among others, in touch with creation, in touch with God." (That's a lot to say, so we put it in code by saying, "Let's hang out.") To say that to a wealthy person may be a way of saying, "I value you for who you are as a person, not what you've achieved in your career or what your money can do for me." But to say that to a socially or economically disadvantaged person is to say something extraordinary. Yet if you cannot say such a thing to someone, there really is no reason in the world she or he should trust you. If you cannot say such a thing to a person, he or she may feel used as a means toward some further end.

Take for example the case of a person who has a terminal illness. This is a time when the *working for* model has little to offer, and the *being with* model is what is most needed. There's very little *working for* to do. Sure, you can fix up all sorts of gadgets and comforts to make the last days or months less burdensome. But there is no way to solve the problem. As for *working with*, there is certainly a lot to be said for demedicalizing the person's situation, for getting away from medical technology meant to prolong life and turning whatever you can into words and mementos and significant moments. But what is really required is simply *being with*—staying still, listening, being silent, not having the answers, sharing the struggle, praying together, singing songs and hymns, taking time over meals, recalling stories, remembering messages to pass on. What is needed is not therapy— it's company. What the dying person is saying is, "Please don't leave me alone."

**Being for.** Let's turn to *being for*. *Being for* may involve becoming very well informed about issues of social inequality and disadvantage. It may mean carefully reading and analyzing local newspapers, participating in blog sites and being familiar with other such vehicles for the formation and exchange of opinion. *Being for* may indicate strongly held convictions, well-researched views and thoughtfully articulated arguments. It may issue in well-phrased letters to newspapers, heated exchanges after seminars or public forums or passionately expressed communications to local leaders or politicians. It frequently entails veiled or demonstrated anger toward those deemed not to live for others—whose lives seem, on the contrary, to be lived egregiously for themselves, as judged by their quantity of possessions, rate of consumption, level of salary or bonuses, treatment of their employees, indifference to the disadvantaged, or maintenance of offensive opinions.

But the fundamental problem with *being for* arises if it becomes clear that all these sophisticated judgments are yet to issue in any kind of significant interpersonal relationship. The tendency of *being for* is to get so wrapped up in sensitivity, tentativeness, theory or reserve, so concerned about having correct views and distancing itself from those with incorrect views, so invested in being knowledgeable about which email petitions to attach one's name to and which products to boycott, that it can end up leaving the socially disadvantaged people as much alone as they would be if the person committed to *being for* had no social concern. Once you've made the journey toward seeing social and economic disadvantage in terms of relationship rather than material wealth, *being for* emerges as a model inadequate on its own.

## THEOLOGICAL APPROACHES TO ENGAGEMENT

Think for a moment about the shape of Jesus' life. Christians usually place a huge emphasis on his last week in Jerusalem—his passion, death and resurrection. That's fully justified, because the Gospels are balanced the same way: Mark gives the last week six chapters out of his sixteen, while John gets to the passiontide material in chapter twelve of his twenty-one chapters. Paul's epistles concentrate almost entirely on Jesus' passion, death and resurrection, and leave Jesus' life out almost altogether.

Before that last week, Jesus spent two, maybe three, years moving around Galilee. In Galilee he built a popular movement. He worked with his disciples, teaching and training them to live in the kingdom he told them was breaking in. He worked with the poor, healing them and empowering them—like the paralyzed man in Mark 2:1-12—to be transformed from burdens on others into carriers of the burdens of others. And he made trouble for the authorities, getting into controversies with those who used their religious and political power for something less than setting God's people free.

We have to assume that, before his ministry in Galilee, Jesus spent around thirty years in Nazareth. Doing what, exactly? Leaving aside the incident when Jesus sat down with the teachers in the temple at the age of twelve, we really have only two verses of Scripture that answer that question. Luke 2:40 says, "The child grew and became strong, filled with wisdom; and the favor of God was upon him," and Luke 2:52 says similar things: "Jesus increased in wisdom and in years, and in divine and human favor."

Before the day the angel Gabriel appeared to the youthful Mary in Nazareth—before the day God in Christ became utterly manifest among us—God had *been for* Israel. God had, in addition, *worked for* Israel in sustaining Israel against imperious enemies and impossible odds. And God had *worked with* Israel through a covenant relationship that spanned many centuries. In some ways God already had a *being with* relationship with Israel—represented by the temple in general and the ark of the covenant in particular. But the incarnation of Jesus expressed the *being* of God *with* us in a way that, while it had always been true for God, was not, before that moment, equally apparent to us. The incarnation marks the moment when God's mode of presence moves definitively from *being for* to *being with*.

If we review Jesus' ministry in the light of the categories

we have been considering in this chapter, the following is what we see.

Jesus spent a week in Jerusalem *working for* us, doing what we can't do, achieving our salvation. If you like, he was the person in the grocery store parking lot who said, "Here, let me carry that burden for you." There were significant *being with* elements (think of the anointing at Bethany in Matthew 26:6-13, Mark 14:3-9 and John 12:1-8) and *working with* elements (there was much disputation with the authorities and formation of the disciples), but the heart of the last week was what Jesus had to do alone.

Jesus spent three years in Galilee *working with* us, calling disciples to follow him and work alongside him. He encouraged and empowered people with their "grocery bags," removing obstacles and reshaping loads, but letting the people themselves determine the direction and claim the credit afterward. For example, he formed and trained the disciples to "do the works that I do and, in fact, . . . do greater works than these" (John 14:12). There were significant *being with* elements, such as the shared meals, and notable *working for* elements, especially the miracles. There were also *being for* elements—we can see Jesus as *being for* the Gentiles and *for* the whole creation, even though his principal focus was the lost sheep of Israel. Nonetheless, this period of ministry was fundamentally characterized by *working with*.

But before Jesus ever got into *working with* and *working for*, he spent thirty years in Nazareth *being with* us, setting aside plans and strategies, and experiencing in his own body not just the exile and oppression of the children of Israel living under the

Romans but also the joy and sorrow of family and community life. We don't know the details of this period, but that silence all the more suggests it was not a time of major *working with* or *working for*, with whose narration the Gospel writers are largely concerned.

A key question to ask is, "To what extent are we prepared to allow Jesus' death and resurrection to be the fundamental *working for* that relativizes all our own attempts to *work for*?" We would love to have the ability to "save" others by securing their temporary, abiding and even eternal well-being, but the Gospels witness that this salvation is something that comes only in the cross and resurrection of Jesus and the sending of the Holy Spirit. Thus all our attempts to *work for*—our attempts that are not short-term, temporary acts of good will—are in danger of masquerading as salvation. *Working with* and *being with* are best understood as enjoying and making more widely available the *working for* that is fundamentally done only by Jesus.

And so the question of how we approach engagement in relation to social disadvantage is fundamentally a question of how we see ourselves before God. The joy of being a child of God is more than anything else the joy of *being with* God—not just *working for* or *with* God but simply *being with* God because there is nowhere better to be.

People often quote these words of Irenaeus: "The glory of God is a human being fully alive." But they generally leave out the words that follow: "And the human life is the vision of God."[8] If Jesus shows us not only what it means to be God but what it means to be human, we should take his example seriously. For

Christian ministry, service and witness, there can be no true *working for* or *working with* God or humanity that is not deeply rooted in *being with* both.

To understand what it might mean to embody Nazareth—to minister, serve and witness in the spirit of *being with*—it may be helpful to consider a very interesting distinction made by Augustine of Hippo. At the start of his book *On Christian Doctrine* he described the difference between what we "use" and what we "enjoy."

> There are some things, then, which are to be enjoyed, others which are to be used, others still which we enjoy and use. Those things which are objects of enjoyment make us happy. Those things which are objects of use assist, and . . . support us in our efforts after happiness, so that we can attain the things that make us happy and rest in them. . . . If we set ourselves to enjoy those [things] which we ought to use, we are hindered in our course, and sometimes even led away from it; so that, getting entangled in the love of lower gratifications, we lag behind in, or even altogether turn back from, the pursuit of the real and proper objects of enjoyment.
>
> For to enjoy a thing is to rest with satisfaction in it for its own sake.[9]

Sin could be understood as "using" what should be "enjoyed" and "enjoying" what should be "used." Too much eagerness to *work for* and solve or fix problems leaves you eager to find things you can "use." Not finding much to use in a neighborhood, or with a person or a number of people in severe distress, can lead you to move on elsewhere in search of more usable material. But the gift of *being with* is learning how to *enjoy* what many predecessors have failed to *use*. When you say, "I'm happy to *be with* you," you're saying, "I am enjoying you"—that's to say (in Augustine's words), "'I am resting in satisfaction with you for your own sake.' You are not a means to any end. You are an end in yourself. I have no purpose in being in this conversation, in this neighborhood, other than to receive from you all the wonder that God brought about just in making you."

Usually people only ever say this to friends on their birthday—"I am rejoicing simply in the gift God gave us in making you." Learning to *be with* is learning to treat people as if every day were their birthday. To minister, serve and witness in a spirit of *being with* means to learn to *enjoy* people for their own sake, not to *use* people and—finding them wanting or unresponsive—get cross with them or toss them away.

Perhaps the most significant way one can embody the ethos of *being with* is to share meals with people. We, the authors, have each discovered something about what it means to share food. We each like the idea of loving others in a *being for*, noncommittal way. But from time to time someone pushes against the safe boundaries of our *being for*. When we have realized we care about someone and want to get to know him or her better, we find ourselves wanting to cook for that person. In other words we each detect a desire to *work for* him or her. When we deeply care about someone, we find we want to cook *with* that person. Somehow the little negotiations over how they or we roast potatoes or sieve flour and who gets to decide when we disagree become the music to which the words of our conversation are sung. This is a regular experience of *working with*.

But when we not only care about someone very much but also know that person very well, the food becomes somehow secondary, and it is really an excuse simply to sit beside each other and listen to each other's voices and spend time in each other's company. The food is something we *use*, so that we can *enjoy* one another. Both of us have found that eating together is the single simplest and most enjoyable way of embodying what it means to move from *being for* to *working for* to *working with* to *being with*.

Here are two quotations that Sam has discovered have sustained him and other people in ministry, particularly in the times when they have sought to *be with* disadvantaged people over long periods and have felt they had little tangible to show for it. The first is from the late Northern Irish pastor Bill Arlow: "It is better to fail in a cause that will finally succeed than to succeed in a cause that will finally fail." So much of *working for* is succeeding in causes that will finally fail: delivering programs that produce good statistics but only reinforce inequalities, launching initiatives that only institutionalize humiliation and making grand statements that only disable genuine relationships. What will finally succeed is years and years of *being with*, building trust, caring about people for their own sake, expecting to see the face of God in them and enjoying them for the wondrous creation that they are. It may not look like much, but it is the way Christ spent most of his incarnate life.

The second comes from the mystic Thomas à Kempis, in his work *The Imitation of Christ*: "That which is done for love (though it be little and contemptible in the sight of the world) becomes wholly fruitful." *Being for* and *working for* may be done for love or for many other reasons. *Working with* may be done for love, though it is possible to have other goals in mind. But *being with*, as far as we can tell, has only one motivation: it is because the other is precious for his or her own sake, solely to be enjoyed, with no thought to use. *Being with* can only be done for love. And in that, it imitates the way God loves us. God is *with* us, Emmanuel, for no other reason than that God loves us for our own sake. God *enjoys* us. That is the mystery of creation and salvation. That is the mystery that all our ministry, service and witness must seek to imitate and emulate. If, and only if, it does, will it become wholly fruitful.

# 2

# Ministry

*Before I came in contact with this wonderful fellowship of peace-loving people, I had already had a thirst for peace. Yet I honestly had no idea where to find it.*

COREY, RE-ENTRY FAITH TEAM PARTNER

*My participation in the re-entry team has become increasingly important to me. It has redirected my priorities and strengthened my faith in and conversations with God. God's grace, forgiveness and love are quite palpable in our partners and members.*

IRA, RE-ENTRY FAITH TEAM MEMBER

his chapter traces the journey of Marcia and the Religious Coalition for a Nonviolent Durham through the four dimensions of social engagement explored in the first chapter. Founded in 1992, the coalition is a nonprofit, interfaith organization whose mission is to rectify and prevent violence through intentional relationships that facilitate both institutional reform and individual acts of compassion and reconciliation. The coalition supports three ministries within the Durham community that invite neighbors to know one another in peaceful covenant: prayer vigils for homicide victims, free monthly community luncheon roundtables, and reconciliation and re-entry ministry teams of newly released prisoners and people of faith. The coalition staff consists of a part-time executive director, Marcia, and a part-time administrator, Judi. Both are also active coalition volunteers.

## DURHAM IS MY NAZARETH

The first step in Marcia's journey was to get to the point of *being for*. The journey to *being for* was a journey to the point of saying, "Gun violence is a major public problem that we all need to address." And this was no small step, because gun violence in the city of Durham is not highly visible.

There are good psychological and political reasons why people might want to keep gun violence invisible. Let's start with the psychological ones. Violence is the moment of rage when a lingering trust in physical or technological force floods the imagi-

nation with an apparently instant solution to an otherwise para-
lyzing powerlessness and fear. It is a desperate attempt to assert
short-term physical control in a situation that is psychologically
out of control. In a spiritual sense, violence is a profound forgetting. It is a forgetting of the past—that I have been created for a
purpose by a God who wholly knows me and at the same time
wondrously, wholly loves me. It is a forgetting of the present—
that I am a child of God, that these others around me are my
brothers and sisters, also created, known and loved by God. And
it is a forgetting of the future—that God is drawing all things
together into a profound and peaceable unity, where there is a
place for everyone in a harmony of God's composing.

How might we describe the opposite of violence? Like this:
"Love me, so that I may love you, so that we may love one another." That's our purpose, that's why we were created, that's
the ticket to profound peace. The peace of God resides in *belong-
ing*, in knowing that we belong to all things, to all people, and
that is our purpose. We were created to love.

If gun violence were more visible, this psychological problem,
the sense of rage and powerlessness and fear, would have to be
owned and addressed by everyone. But the wider society has
reached a consensus around two incompatible convictions. One
is that those with this psychological problem are a tiny minority,
and they can be disregarded by the majority of the population
because they are assumed to be of a specific class and race other
than the majority's own—and thus assigned to a category that
is *"not us."*

The other conviction is that we all, nonetheless, need a gun.

During her many years of involvement with the problem of gun violence, Marcia has seen over and over how and why people say, "I need a gun. By asking me to disarm, you are putting me at risk." But having a gun is not a solution. We have gone so far from Christ's teachings that we see ourselves as being separate from one another. One way not to have a problem is to deny the problem by saying, "It's not *my* problem. I have a house, and I'm going to get a security system, and I'm going to get a weapon, so that I'm ready to kill someone"—a person who is in reality my brother or sister—"so that I can save my life." So, what in us makes us reluctant to call gun violence our problem? Fear, and a forgetting of our soul.

The political dimensions of why people might want to keep gun violence invisible are not so subtle. No one wants to live in a town with a homicide rate that ranks with Detroit's or Miami's. This is not the image that Durham wants for itself or the image that prestigious Duke University, whose campus is on the west side of the city, close to downtown, wants to offer to prospective students, their parents or possible new faculty. If this gun violence is restricted to a tiny segment of the population, so the logic goes, there is no need to portray it as some kind of epidemic.

This was Marcia's reaction when she first became aware of the political dimension of the problem. It was 1992. The homicide victims were, overwhelmingly, young African Americans in their twenties and teens. What enraged her so much was that their deaths were being recorded deep inside the Metro section of the newspaper, among the local crime reports, buried far from the front page, along with assorted mundane and ephemeral events. The loss of life in this community—a tiny community compared to Washington, D.C., where Marcia had been living—was, to her, flabbergasting.

For Marcia the journey to *being for* was a personal one as well as a social and political one. The personal dimension interwove with the more public concerns. She had grown up as a white person in a segregated Durham, but in 1970 the city schools were integrated and she was assigned to the historically black Hillside High School. It is hard for those in the privileged class, in the dominant race, segregated from those who are oppressed, exploited, neglected and abused by racism, truly to know how racism manifests itself. But Hillside put Marcia in physical proximity to it. She could see the way the school was compared to Durham High, where her older brother had gone. It wasn't always easy at Hillside, or even amicable. But people were getting on with life. There would be fights, but nobody ever went to the hospital.

So, when Marcia came home to Durham eleven years later, in 1988, after graduating from high school and college, she knew that we can have economic inequality, we can have segregation, we can have racism, sexism and other toxic attitudes and realities in a community—but people don't have to die. And yet she would read the paper and be astounded: every other week someone was being shot and killed. For Marcia, the finality of those violent and preventable deaths was profound.

Marcia had become aware of death in a very personal way since she had left Durham. Her best friend had contracted HIV, and she began living with the possibility of his death. It put everything in perspective. She discovered the paradox that when we address and acknowledge and honor death, we become alive. The key to her journey was to realize that gun violence is like AIDS. We run from them and hide them and deny them for the same reason: "If I get near this, maybe it will happen to me. If I get involved in this problem, maybe it will kill *me*."

Marcia had become a mother in that time away from Durham too, and so she had been given the great opportunity to experience both life and death. Both informed her about powerlessness. This was a second paradox: the more she realized she had no power, the more she had all the power in the world. Letting go of her desire to control allowed her to hear God. And in hearing God, she found the significance of her insignificance.

This is the disposition that has been most foundational to the work of the Religious Coalition for a Nonviolent Durham: living beyond fear. It means hearing God say, *"Love,* just *love.* Find your way to love that person, find your way to love that forest, find your way to love all things, especially the things you find so unlovable and so frightening." God did not create this world to frighten you. God did not create this world for you to starve or for you to be afraid or for you to suffer. That doesn't mean that we should see suffering and hurt as separate from God, but rather that it's all there to heal, it's all there for us to understand. And in that understanding, love is made possible. Marcia came back to Durham with that kind of understanding. She simply said, "I surrender. I surrender to these profound truths of life and death." She found a humility that overcomes fear and replaces it with love.

Looking back, what strikes Marcia most is how easily her growing *being for* convictions became harnessed to *working for* assumptions. The compassion that was emerging from the integration of her personal history and some intense life experiences was quickly overtaken by a number of paternalistic modes of operation. In the early years of the Religious Coalition for a Nonviolent Durham, she found herself in the company of a group of people stirred by *being for* convictions, and together they were captivated by *working for* habits and ideas.

Then she and the coalition members realized who was dying. Those dying weren't affluent white people. They were primarily African Americans, many of whom were from families that had experienced generations of material poverty. The group's response to that realization was to assume that what it needed to do was to create policy. Durham needed laws to prohibit the presence of guns in as many locations as possible. That means working with local officials to pass gun ordinances. The ordinances would mean people could still buy guns, but they couldn't carry them in funeral processions, public parks, public buildings and so on. In the beginning, that's what the coalition was really about: getting legislation on the books that would reduce the proliferation of guns, because the more guns there were, the more injuries and deaths would occur.

Imagine a mother's point of view. She's on a playground, and she's watching children play. A child picks up a stick and walks toward another child, preparing to whack the playmate with it. The mother's immediate, primary concern is the children's safety, so she intervenes by taking away the stick. That was Marcia's attitude: a *working for* attitude. She recalls thinking, "In the same way, I'm going to intercede on behalf of my community to prevent guns from finding their way into the hands of our children and other unauthorized people." She and others spent hours, days, months, years among lawmakers, advocating for sensible gun laws that would protect lives—especially the lives of children.

One of the first opportunities to help prevent gun injuries and deaths, especially of law-enforcement officers, was to advocate for the federal assault weapons ban. Marcia called dozens of people in Durham about the legislation, asking them to call their representatives in favor of the ban. It passed. Other ordinances passed as well. And it seemed that the new laws would be effective.

Then, a few years later, the National Rifle Association (NRA) lobbied successfully for a state preemption law. When a state wants to preempt a local municipality's law, it usually replaces the local law with another law. In this case, the state passed preemption laws that said that every municipality—county, township, city—was prohibited from regulating gun sales, gun shows, gun distribution, gun retail. And any laws that might be on the books became null and void. No law was replaced, only eliminated. This especially affected the metropolitan areas where people were being shot in the streets—like Durham. So Marcia and the coalition found the rug ripped out from under their feet. There was no longer an outlet for local policymaking.

It took this resistance from the NRA and others to stir the Religious Coalition for a Nonviolent Durham into different models of engagement. But as Marcia looks back on the *working for* era of the coalition's existence, she sees that its aims and methods would have been profoundly flawed *even if they had proved to be legislatively successful.* That is because *working for* models are not capable of getting to the root of these kinds of problems. In this particular case, this was true for two main reasons.

First of all, laws that address guns primarily address the problem through increasing punishment. For instance, laws in Durham could say, "We will deal with gun violence by adding five more years in prison for possession of a firearm." But while these laws could punish people more and more strictly for carrying firearms, what they could not do was to ask why there were so many guns in cities like Durham in the first place. Laws focused on prohibition and punishment are not accompanied by a comparable investment in the prevention of gun violence, because there is not adequate regulation of the design, production, retail and distribution of firearms. A brand-new pistol, in the box, costs $50 in Durham. To suggest that manufacturers don't know where their weapons are selling and how they're selling and what they're selling for is disingenuous. So this was the first key problem the coalition discovered: the legislative approach was primarily working on punishment rather than prevention. And the people being punished were overwhelmingly young African American men—many of whom came from families deeply rooted in material poverty. The *working for* approach, focused as it was on restricting guns in public places, was not addressing the questions of who was bearing the brunt of the punishment of, and losses from, gun violence.

This leads to the second and, perhaps, more crucial problem:

the coalition's methods up to this point had focused on the courts and the lawmakers, rather than on the families most directly affected by gun violence and gun laws. As we will see, this realization led to profound shifts in the way the coalition approached the problem of gun violence. The coalition did not let go of its commitment to working within the legal system through lobbying and advocacy for better laws. But the coalition now realized it was time to explore other models of engagement as well.

## THE JOURNEY FROM "FOR" TO "WITH"

Gradually the coalition began to explore approaches that bore a closer resemblance to *working with*. Perhaps the best example of this came when Marcia and others decided it was time to confront the newspaper editors whose decisions about the relative unimportance of gun-related deaths had initially sparked her rage. One of the many facets of the injustice of gun violence was how the deaths were being reported. So the coalition decided, "One thing we *can* do is invite the editor of the local newspaper to come speak with us." When they met, everyone was very polite, but the editor kept saying, "I'm just doing my job; it's my job to report these incidences, and it's important to give that information."

So Marcia looked at him and said, "Are you saying that if my child, my son, got shot and killed, you would publish that story on the third page of the Metro section?" And the editor said, without missing a beat, "Oh no!" There was a united gasp. Nobody knew what to say or do. Everyone just looked at him, and he said, "Oh, I get it." From that time forward, the newspapers changed the way they report these deaths.

What the coalition realized was that the way a community tells its story, the way a community reports its incidences and news, has the power to shape the community's perception of an issue. The way deaths were being reported could either deflect attention from certain deaths (the deaths of "marginal" people) or could treat every death, in all its complexity, as an equal loss and tragedy within the community. What the community needed was more information about the whole situation, rather than a simple criminalization of the victim. The coalition began to meet with reporters, and they met regularly with the newspaper's editorial board. They gathered a group of doctors, public policy advocates and community activists, and gave them resources so that it would be easy for them to report on the factors involved in deaths from gun violence. With access to this kind of information, it was hoped that people could no longer say, "This is not my problem." Instead the approach sought to help everyone in Durham say, "This is our community, and we need to know all the parts of this problem so that we can address it."

The coalition was inching toward a more collaborative *working with* model of engagement. But still the people in the room when the conversation was taking place were largely experts— doctors, public policy advocates, community activists. So a true *working with* model was not yet in the coalition's imagination. Meanwhile, the beginnings of a *being with* approach were appearing, but with some significant blind spots still in evidence.

The coalition now saw violence as a spiritual problem, as well as a social, racial, economic and civil rights problem. It had been gathering for a luncheon meeting every fourth Thursday of the month since 1992. In 1997, a young woman at the meeting said, "Why don't we have prayer vigils at the sites of the homicides?" And everyone looked at each other and said, "Okay!" It seemed profoundly the right thing to do. There wasn't even much discussion. David, the executive director of the umbrella organization, Durham Congregations in Action, said, "I'll do it."

And that was the start of a new era. David began contacting families of homicide victims, and members of the coalition would go to the homicide sites and pray. The coalition was still trying to work with legislation, but now they were meeting the families who lived with the reality and aftermath of gun violence. In retrospect, it seems unthinkable to coalition members that they had gotten so far without being in contact with the victims' loved ones.

But these *working for* assumptions happen everywhere, on any issue. If you investigate who's working on an issue, often it's a bunch of people who have no personal experience with the problem, who are as clear as crystal that they know exactly what to do, *because they've studied it.* Now the professionals and habitual compassion givers—the *being for* and *working for* aficionados— were gradually beginning to realize that the families and the people at the heart of the issue had some information, some perspective, some wisdom that the experts were beginning to find they genuinely needed.

Marcia's moment of transformation came at a vigil in 2002. Until that point, her imagination had still been in *for* mode— constantly urgent, constantly seeking solutions, constantly thinking over the heads of the families themselves and seeking to act on their behalf. But that began to change the night of one particularly memorable and significant vigil. For the first time, the true dimensions of *being with* began to emerge.

The vigil was led by a local pastor named Joe. It was downtown, a couple of blocks from the public library and from Joe's church. A man named James had been shot, and to get away from the bullets he had jumped through a window and been cut, and he died. Mourners were standing there, and it was dark—it was in the wintertime. The neighbors were all gathered at the vigil, talking about the great things James had done for them. He was a *good* man who gave of himself for others, they all said.

Then Marcia spotted two young men walking down the street. She left the group, approached them and said, "Come and join us." And they said, "What are you doing?" Marcia told them, and they joined the group—much to her surprise. At the end of Joe's closing prayer, one of the young men said, "This is good. This is good, what you're doing. Keep doing it—this is a good thing. Thank you." Then they walked away. And the woman next to Marcia said, "They're just coming home from prison. They just got left off at the courthouse, and they're walking home."

About six weeks later, Marcia learned from a friend that the city's most recent homicide was the young man at the vigil who had affirmed and encouraged them. He hadn't said, "You crazy people, what are you doing in my neighborhood?" He'd understood that they were where they were supposed to be, doing what they were supposed to do. And that discovery brought Marcia to her knees. It broke her heart open, and she realized that *it isn't about victims—is about all of us.* It broke her heart to see that she had become hardened to the perpetrators. Being in fellowship with victims, the suffering and sorrow and loss is so immeasurable that it becomes hard not to feel angry and want to punish the people who did it. But, as Marcia realized, that is not the way of Christ.

This is how the coalition changed—through being present with the victims and feeling their hearts harden toward the offenders. And then when this young man was killed, that huge illusion shattered. It was an "aha" moment. God came and reminded Marcia not to make distinctions. Jesus didn't say, "Only love your neighbors that you approve of, only love your neighbors who behave the way you want them to, only love the neighbors who look like you, talk like you, make the same amount of money you do, and certainly, above all else, believe the way you do." So Marcia felt a gift being given to her—the awareness that we are a profound unity; we are of equal value and worth.

Fully receiving this gift took about two more years. Marcia started to seek God in the presence of and in fellowship with people who were coming home from prison. Once that happened, the crucial step followed. She found out—whether she hadn't heard it before because she couldn't hear it or because people weren't telling her—that within some of the victims' families, there were people in prison. And some of them were in prison for shooting people. She realized her own eagerness to make judgments prevented her from seeing the whole picture, and that meant that she was inhibiting, rather than helping, the families who were striving to be whole. It was a huge conversion. It was a conversion into *being with*.

What Marcia realized was that even when things may look really bad, and there may be injustice abounding, God still offers us everything we need to *be with* one another, everything we need to be God's presence in the world. She hadn't been able to see that she was going in and judging, saying, "You're in, and you're out. Victims are in, and perpetrators are out." But once she realized that was not what God intended for her, she discovered an extraordinary liberation. It allowed her to love. She could feel her soul grow. It didn't change her personality—it didn't erase all the hurts and the fears and the anxieties she had. But it let her *love*. And it gave her peace.

This was the transformation everyone who makes the journey from *working for* to *being with* has to accept. If you are going to change the world, you have to be willing for the world to change you. The kingdom lies as much in the beauty of allowing yourself to be changed as it does in the desire to see others change.

Marcia charts this change in a more direct way in relation to her own history as a student and a businesswoman. Over the years of being involved in the coalition, she has gone from a primarily public policy perspective to a largely personal one. She wanted to engage with the lives of people who are *affected* by gun violence, the families of homicide victims, and then she wanted to engage with the lives of people who are perpetrating it—hence the emergence of the reconciliation and re-entry ministry, which partners local congregation members with people recently released from prison. In the process, she realized that the distinction between victim and perpetrator can sometimes be false.

Solutions—whether social, political or economic—are the most fruitful when they come from relationships that encompass a variety of people in a community, most importantly the people who are the most personally impacted by the issue. Too often the *working for* mindset assumes that the people who are personally affected are the least qualified people to inform public policy. It says, "These people are *damaged* by the problem, so they can't . . . " as opposed to saying, "These people are *suffering* from the problem, so they also will have the best insight into resolving the problem."

Marcia always enjoyed science. For her it meant articulating questions and describing them *ad infinitum* until the answer "popped." In contrast, the greatness and the power and the promise of diverse relationships within a community is that people together can describe in a complete and whole way what the problem is—instead of one person or group circumventing those who are most personally impacted, deciding what needs to be done, implementing change and then walking away. That's what Marcia's path originally was: not so much walking away, but thinking, "Oh, that will take care of it; that will fix the problem." She learned that what people of faith are especially called to do is to be *in* the problem, to *be with* the problem—to expect transformation and to expect to be transformed through that process. That's where the kingdom lies.

Augustine's distinction between using and enjoying, which we noted near the end of the first chapter, is exactly the point at issue here. As long as *working for* assumptions persisted, the victims of gun violence and their families were always liable to be *used* to fix a problem that lay fundamentally in law or public policy. The shift to *being with* families was a recognition that the families were to be *enjoyed* as they were and for their own sake, and if social transformation of a legal or policy nature was going to occur, it would need to be led by them.

## THE QUALITIES OF BEING WITH

It is relatively easy to describe what *being with* is not. The following is what we've discovered being with *is*.

More than anything else, *being with* means presence. The vigil ministry has taught us that you don't have to do anything but be present. The first thing most people tend to want to do about a problem is figure it out and solve it. The vigil ministry showed that this is the least appropriate response. It's not that solving problems is not part of ministry. It's that the first reaction should not be to assume you are meeting a problem ripe for solving and to conclude, "I am the person best placed to solve this." It's an illusion, a grand illusion, that we can "fix" anything without God, that we can pass a law, change the zoning, make a new tax, build more prisons—whatever our feeble, scared imaginations come up with. The whole approach effectively excludes God.

The most significant thing about presence is that it breaks down the separation that assumes we can know the answer without needing to enter into the suffering person's experience. We think, "This is terrible, we've got to change this." But how do we know what to change unless we have physically, spiritually and emotionally entered the lives of the people who are suffering the most? Is it not profound arrogance to think any one person would know what to do to alleviate the suffering of others without being in any proximity to those who suffer? What Marcia found through friendships with people—families of homicide victims, folks coming home from prison, children involved with gangs—is that *they* are the answer. There is no longer a distinction between *they* and *we*. *We* become the answer—all of us together.

One of the gifts that emerges from a commitment to presence is the recognition of abundance. For Marcia, the discovery of abundance has arisen through a sustained experience of being present in the face of death. The vigils can be times of profound scarcity, particularly when there is no one present who knew the murdered person. At those times there is an uncomfortable element of *being for*, because the vitality of relationships is missing. But much more often the vigils are an experience of abundance in the face of the scarcity of violence and death. Marcia's philosophy is that when she goes *toward* something that she desperately wants to retreat from, that's always the right choice. It's those things that she fears the most that she needs to get to know the best. She has discovered that when she is around a lot of death and around people in mourning and lament, God is especially visible. The only response to immeasurable loss is God's immeasurable love.

The conversation at the vigils discloses a great deal. What people talk about is how much they loved the person who died and what the person did for others. In all the countless vigils, what people say is, "He fixed my porch." "He let me sleep on his couch." "She always let me in." "She always fed me." "He always made me laugh." "He loved us." People express their love for the person who's been killed by describing how their loved one, the victim, loved them. You never hear people say, "We did this for him." You just hear, "We love him so much. This is what he did for us."

When they talk about the love between them and the person who died, what they describe is care, attention and acceptance. Care for physical needs, emotional needs, spiritual needs, financial needs. If you ever want to know what matters, that's it. You learn it all in a vigil. You learn what matters, what endures, what is eternal and infinite. And it is very concrete. The witness of these beloved families teaches others present how to live.

Being present has taught Marcia about abundance in a way she could never otherwise have known. This has led her to the discovery that *being with* is precisely the opposite of violence, for *being with* means living without enemies. In the words of Henry Wadsworth Longfellow, "If we could read the secret history of our enemies, we should find in each man's life sorrow and suffering enough to disarm all hostility." Marcia's personal experience met her political awakening around exactly this theme.

Marcia discovered in prayer that God has no enemies. To be sure, Scripture describes death as an enemy to be destroyed by God (1 Corinthians 15:26) and the devil as an adversary (Romans 16:20; 1 Peter 5:8). But when it comes to human beings, God views no person as an enemy but rather as a beloved child, God's own creation, made to be in relationship with God. People can make themselves enemies of God (James 4:4), but God never makes enemies out of people.

This changed her outlook on everything. Jesus says, "Love

God, love yourself and love your neighbor." He doesn't say, "Love the neighbor who looks like you, love the neighbor who believes like you." He says, "Love your neighbor." And in this big beautiful world, that means all of us. How can any one of us do that? Only by recognizing that we're all children of God, we're all created by God. This made Marcia wonder, *Why would I have an enemy? What makes someone an enemy?* Marcia has been able, through others' acceptance of her, to discover that when she acts like an enemy toward someone else, it is a result of her own sorrow and suffering.

What makes a person lash out and make someone an enemy? It comes from a feeling of profound powerlessness and fear that says, "I'm not big enough for this." Living without enemies is radical acceptance. It is taking a moment, just a moment, to sink your head into your heart—or to lead with your soul and let your mind follow. You lead with your soul by taking a moment to say, "I accept all that is, all the suffering I've caused, all the suffering I've endured. I just accept it. There are no enemies." Then you can begin to see the glorious nature of each one of us. You can see the potential.

This led Marcia to feel God's arms wrapping around her and cradling her in a profound safety, and God saying, "Everything—*everything*—you need is right here, now." Marcia takes that consciousness and puts it in the context of meeting with families who are in enormous, immeasurable sorrow. And when she is reminded that it's all here, everyone and everything they need, she discovers the most empowering gift in ministry: hearing God whispering, "I have no enemies."

The archetypal *working for* approach is to remove or disable or even destroy enemies on others' behalf, or at least to limit the damage enemies can do. The characteristic *working with* approach is either to join forces to overcome enemies together or to enlarge the group, so that those who previously might have been enemies become partners in a larger cause. But the *being with* philosophy is to hear God whispering, "I have no enemies." This is a plea to see every relationship as a manifestation of the Holy Spirit.

What Marcia discovered in learning to live without enemies is that the heart of justice is mercy. And that is precisely the place where *being with* resides. Justice is unimaginable without mercy. The heart of mercy is God, who has no enemies. Justice begins when you stop judging. As Marcia often says, "If I can't see me in you, if I can't know and experience that you belong to me and I belong to you—that what happens to you in fact happens to me—then I can't know justice." Because then it's simply about power. And that's not where God resides.

So *being with* in the face of gun violence means a commitment to presence and the discovery of abundance and the primacy of mercy and the need to live without enemies. One final dimension of *being with* is implied by all these things: the transcendence of fear. This brings the themes of this chapter full circle. We began by suggesting that fear is at the heart of violence. We conclude by proposing that the final response to violence is learning to live without fear. If fear leads to violence, learning to live without enemies means turning from fearing others to loving them. As we've already seen, love is at the heart of *being with*— and love drives out fear (1 John 4:18).

Marcia discovered what it means to live beyond fear one dark winter evening, when she was taking some food to Tony, one of the coalition's re-entry faith team partners, a man who was seeking help to live a nonviolent life after a period of incarceration. Tony and April had just had little Tony Junior, and they needed food. There had just been a homicide and a subsequent vigil near the place where they lived. Marcia knew the neighborhood through the vigil ministry, so she called Robert, her husband, to tell him she was going to be late because she was dropping off some food for Tony and April.

As she said, "Bye, honey," she was looking for Tony's house and driving very slowly. She put down the phone, and then she saw a man standing by the side of the street, whom she thought was Tony. So she rolled her window down, and said, "Tony?" The next thing she knew, the man was in her car. He didn't smell great, and he looked stressed. But Marcia thought, "Oh, here's my *brother!*"

She immediately put her hand out, and said, "Hey, I'm Marcia. What's your name?" His response was, "Drive!" She said, "Okay, all right, let's go." Many assumptions about his intentions filled her mind, yet none was greater than the realization that he needed her. So she started saying, "What do you need? Do you have a family? I would love to help you. What can I do?" He wanted money, and Marcia said, "No problem, I have some. Here's twenty dollars." And they drove by Tony, who was standing on the side of the road, saying, "Whoa! Wait a minute!"

It wasn't that Marcia wasn't afraid—she was startled, alarmed—but she never lost sight of her own sacred humanity, or his. She said, "I'm going to take you back now," and he argued with her about it, but she said, "No, no, you need to get home, and if you need anything, I'd love to give you my number. You can call me anytime, because I know your kids need you, and I have a family too." And she dropped him off.

The man got out of the car and walked away. Suddenly, she saw Tony a few yards up the street. He said to her, "What on earth are you doing?" Marcia told him what was going on, and he said, "You could have gotten yourself killed."

On the way home, Marcia thought to herself, *I can't tell Robert this. I want to tell Robert this, but if I tell him, he'll never let me out again.* So she got home, and Robert said, "So, busy night?" She breathed in, and said, "Well, yeah, this really incredible thing . . . " He interrupted and said, "Yes, I know, I listened to the whole thing on the phone." Marcia suddenly realized that she'd never cut the call off after she'd said goodbye. She thought, *Okay, I'm in big trouble.* She assumed Robert's fear would kick in.

Robert looked at her and said, "I will never be afraid again." That was his response. He chuckled as he recalled the man's comment—"Most white women would be scared to death right now"—and recalled how flummoxed the man had sounded. Then Robert said, "That was an act of God. It was terrifying. I didn't know if I should get off the phone and call the police. I didn't know what to do, so I just stayed on the phone. But," he said, "Marcia, God is real. I will never fear again."

What had begun as a movement to legislate against the gun had led after many years to the discovery of what it means to live beyond fear—of violence, of guns, of death itself.

# 3

# Silence

*Imagine the lives that could and would be saved if any and every person who has had a violent upbringing or has simply seen too much in their lives had someone to turn to whenever they felt they were going to lose sight of the importance of peace.*

COREY, RE-ENTRY FAITH TEAM PARTNER

*I believe that things will start to change when we really begin to see each other as brothers and sisters. When we begin to honestly feel that we are all part of the same community—not just residents of separate neighborhoods—then we will begin to find the grief and pain and loss caused by violence to be truly unacceptable, and we will join together to finally say, Enough is enough. The coalition is one opportunity for people to get out of their comfort zones and to join real community. There are other opportunities, and we need to find them, to take advantage of them and to create new ones. And if you do, you will feel the rewards in your life.*

RON, RE-ENTRY FAITH TEAM MEMBER

*I*n chapter two, we identified the heart of *being with* as the commitment to remain present in spite of enmity and fear. We spoke about how enmity and fear are usually overwhelming barriers to forging and maintaining relationships with those living under the shadow of gun violence. This and the next two chapters explore three dimensions of being present: silence, touch and words.

We have also described how Marcia came to recognize the damage being brought about in her community by gun violence. It was destroying families, it was keeping children inside, it was terrifying, it was making people hypervigilant. The troubled neighborhood was no longer somewhere "over there" for Marcia. It was where her friends lived and where her friends' children lived—children she grew to love. Suddenly to know that her neighborhood was essentially safe and quiet and secure while her friends' neighborhood was not had been deeply disturbing to her. It became *her* problem, not just intellectually but also emotionally and spiritually.

But Marcia couldn't have reached that point if she hadn't been willing just to go there, and spend time there, with no agenda. It was *being with*—time to be together, so that when emergencies came up, they could handle them together. She wasn't there just to be a taxi or for when there were emergencies. She was there to *be with*—to live, to hang out, to pass time, to enjoy people for their own sake.

All the personal and political dimensions of gun violence

surfaced simply through a commitment to *be present* to people in times of fear and danger. This chapter focuses on the silent dimension of that being present—the things that emerge not through explicit action or conversation, but largely through wordless presence.

One key element of the coalition's ministry is the prayer vigil. Prayer vigils are a ministry of presence and place, rather than of performance. They invite the community to gather at the site of the murder, or at a place of meaning for the family and friends of the person slain, for a time of commemoration, grieving, prayer and silence. Most vigils last about thirty minutes. The aim is to recognize publicly the human worth of the victim and the perpetrator, to comfort family and friends and to sanctify and bring healing to the site where the violence occurred. A vigil requests nothing more than willingness to be present and receptive to God's mercy.

For some vigils, only a few people gather; for others, a crowd of witnesses forms. A minister, lay leader, imam or rabbi presides and begins the vigil by inviting everyone to gather. There is no amplification, so everyone stands close together. The faith leader offers condolences to the family, an opening prayer and a reflection. Then those who knew the victim are invited to share their memories, stories or whatever they would like to offer the group. There may be a song sung, relatives introduced, a circle formed to gather the children within, a lesson given, a testimony of tears declared or a description of the victim's signature ways of bringing laughter and solace. This witness is born in the freedom of complete acceptance. When silence returns, the members of the community are invited to offer their reflections, condolences, grief. Then silence comes again, and the vigil leader closes with prayer.

There are no right or wrong expressions of faith, lament or relationship. The quiet inclusiveness of a vigil inevitably guides those present into one another's arms with a gentle passion that concludes almost every vigil.

## SILENCE AS SOLIDARITY

When families talk about the vigils afterward, they seldom refer to what was said and only occasionally speak of what was done. Instead, they say, "Thank you for being here." What they recognize is presence. They say, in essence, "It really meant a lot that there were people outside the family and friends who were here, who recognized our tragedy. And, more importantly, who recognized the significance of my beloved's life." There are no words. There's nothing that the members of the coalition can do. They can't bring the person back. All they can do is be present. Yet in that standing still and being still, their presence does say something. It says, "I offer you my soul. I am here to offer you my life." A remarkable strength comes from that.

The silence of solidarity is a stance against withdrawal. The common problem of all the *being for* or *working for* responses is that they can collude with an impulse to withdraw emotionally—to avoid being present in the place of pain among the people experiencing that pain. The host of explanations for why people get shot and killed—it's poverty, it's racism, it's the educational system, it's the parents' fault, it's a bunch of drug addicts, it's just criminals killing criminals—are all, in the end, justifications for such withdrawal. And so presence is in itself a form of protest against such explanations and such legitimized withdrawal. Marcia's reaction was, "But I can't *not* do this. How can I let people be slain in my town, and no one from the faith community, *no one* who claims Christ as their Savior, is calling these families, saying, 'I'm really sorry. We're really sorry. We recognize that this is not God's intention, that this is a sign that something is profoundly out of balance.'" There is, in the end, nothing people of faith can do except be present with God's light.

At the root of this is a simple but profound theological conviction: Does God *ever* withdraw? *Never.* Does God ever not affirm you and love you and see the perfection in you? Never! Never. Hence presence is a witness of solidarity with those who suffer, but most of all, it is a visible statement that God *does not withdraw* from us out of fear, revulsion, horror or anger and that God never retreats behind familiar explanations or weary blame as a reason to leave us alone.

To stay still is to drop the assumption that you have the solution. It is to rest in the knowledge that you cannot show love independent of relationship and that—obvious as it may seem—the most important dimension of relationship is simple presence. Marcia made a very similar journey in relation to God that she made in relation to the families of the homicide victims. Rather than maintain a relationship characterized entirely by distance and advice, she developed a relationship of presence and silent solidarity. She has found that the vigil ministry changed her understanding of prayer.

Having spent her lifetime talking *to* God, *asking* God for this and that and the other, Marcia has learned *that's not faith*. Simply to tell God what you want God to do is open, honest, transparent and ingenuous. But it's similar to thinking you know what to do about a problem you're not even touching, that you're not really in relationship with. It's assuming *working for* is the only model for God and the only model for us too. Now, when Marcia prays, she just says, "I'm here. I'm here. And thank you." She has enormous gratitude—infinite gratitude. "Thank you . . . thank you . . . thank you. Life is beautiful. Life is wondrous. Thank you for this enormous mystery and abundant love." And then she stops the words and listens.

The silence of solidarity is the most important thing the vigils are about. In this silence there are no answers, only companionship. There are no explanations, only humility. There is no blame, only common humanity. But that silence of solidarity takes discipline, self-knowledge and many years of practice, because it runs counter to a great many instincts and social conventions. Often we want to *speak* because we don't want to *feel*. And sometimes we speak to try to *stop people from feeling*.

At one vigil, a young woman, very upset, said, "Just let me have my feelings." This is now the ethos of the vigil: "Let people feel. Be silent. Don't try desperately to find the words that make it all better. That's not making it all better. That's anxiety trying to get far away, to stop the pain. Instead recognize that there is pain, and go toward it with all of God's strength and love, wisdom and grace." It is a hard discovery. It takes years and years of practice.

Words and gestures may come later. But the heart of the vigils lies here: withholding speech in order to be still and to be present and to allow God to speak and to permit feelings to do what they need to do. This is the time people offer their souls: when they're not talking, when they're not trying to communicate anything. They're not taking the mystical unknowable that we live in and stopping it with words.

In the vigil, sometimes no one says anything, and people are standing together, stranger with stranger, family member with sometimes estranged family member, neighbors who kind of know each other, but maybe not—this unusual but wonderful collection of people. When everyone stops and stands in that silence together, their souls knit together. It is about offering our loves and our souls, and *letting our lives come later.* That is a beautiful time, because it creates the moments for God. There are really no words, because there's nothing to say. The people surrender to their sorrow; they surrender to their inability to change what is. And they surrender to their inability to love. It's the silence that speaks God's truth. It lets God speak.

But there is also a very practical dimension to the silence of solidarity. And that is *being with* families of victims at moments when they would otherwise feel very much alone and vulnerable. It is being there to affirm that they may indeed be vulnerable, but they are not alone. Marcia discovered how important it is to accompany families to meetings with the assistant district attorney. In the criminal justice system, homicide is not a crime against the family. It's not a crime against a neighborhood or community. It's a crime against the state. So the family can be pushed to the side. They're represented by the district attorney's office. They don't have their own lawyer.

When family members are already in deep grief and are required to talk in detail about the worst, most unimaginable thing that has ever happened to them, for them to be able to be analytical and to think clearly is very challenging. Hence the importance of accompanying families. All that's needed is to promise not to say anything. Solidarity means being there not to interrupt, but instead to listen to what is being said—and perhaps what is not being said—and, with the family's permission, to summarize what has been heard during the meeting. That then gives the district attorney or the family the opportunity to say, "You got it all wrong." So the role is not to intercede, but to be interpreters.

This takes us to another dimension of silence: the silence of listening.

## SILENCE AS LISTENING

How do you learn to convey silence as listening, rather than shyness, awkwardness or aloofness? You have to learn to use your eyes, your posture, your attention, your breathing. This kind of silence is a kind of patient waiting. It is waiting for the other person to indicate how things are to be, a waiting that never hints you have something better to be doing, a waiting that should not make the other person feel awkward, because it is fundamentally a waiting on God. Just as the shop assistant learns how to be present while always making the customers feel they are the decision makers, so the patient listener is fully present and attentive to the words and gestures of the other person without seeking to direct them.

This visible, silent waiting says something that otherwise would need to be affirmed in words or gestures, at a time when words and gestures are bound to be faltering and tentative. What it says is this: "This moment in one another's company, this gathering, this conversation, could be *the most important one of your life*. It doesn't have to be. But it *can* be. It may not be the right time for you, but it's *always* the right time for me. I am not going to tell you I'm too busy. I am not going to make light of your struggles. I am not going to tell you something more interesting actually happened to me. I am not going to say, 'I know,' when you're exploring a feeling for the first time. I am not going to change the subject when you bring up something that's hard to hear. I am not going to do any of those things, because all of them in different ways are saying, 'I'm out of my depth.' And what the silent waiting is saying is, 'I am someone who, however deep you wish to go, will never be out of my depth. You can trust me to listen. You can trust me to withhold my personal investment in the issues for another time and another place. You can trust me to be alert to the ways of God, however strange the story you tell. You can trust me to know when some kind of specialized help from another party may be in order. But you can also trust me to know that *now* could be the time more than any other time for the moment of truth.'"

These are the qualities the silence of being present requires. This is the covenant made in the silence of solidarity. This is what it means to acknowledge that we want to speak because we don't want to feel, and we speak to stop people from feeling. The ministry of silence is the opening out of a sabbath place in a world of urgency and demands. It is a still place, a moment 1 Kings 19:12 calls a "sound of sheer silence."

That is the vigil ministry: staying still. It is calling the family after their loved one has died and saying, "We want to honor your beloved with our presence," and then staying still. Every vigil is different, but they usually last thirty minutes; periods of silence within them might last a minute at a time. Staying still requires embodying and expressing many paradoxes. It means living in the knowledge that everything we need, everything, all the goodness, is here, now. You can only really get that when you're still. When you're busy, when you're going from point A to point B, when you have an agenda, the faster you go and the more judgmental you become, the more determined you are that your perception of reality will prevail.

Those who learn this stillness find that their lives become a sabbath for those who encounter them. Their lives become a reminder that God works while we sleep, and so those who meet them can receive permission to rest. Their lives become an embrace of the qualities and the gifts in those around them that others have been too busy or too threatened or too self-absorbed to see and encourage. Their lives become an invitation into a place of depth, but an exhilarating invitation because it is depth without fear, depth as an adventure in which you are expecting to be met by God. Their lives become a place and a time of renewal in which others rediscover who they are and who God is.

And they can be almost all of these things without ever saying one word. This is the power of silence.

## SILENCE AS PRAYER

Silence has three dimensions. The first is solidarity: enjoying the wordless presence of another person as a stronghold in times of despair, distress and fear. It means believing that being present is more important than well-chosen words or sensitive actions.

The second dimension is listening: the giving of permission for those in distress to discover things they didn't already know by articulating them in their own time and in their own way without judgment or interruption. Those who are present in the silence of listening are there not as experts who know what to do but as witnesses to share a discovery. This dimension of silence recognizes that there are sighs too deep for words.

The third dimension is the silence of prayer. The first dimension says, "This is about us, together. We're with you in this." The second dimension says, "I realize this is really about you. I'm here to listen to your experience and the wisdom you have found in that." The third dimension says, "This whole experience was and is always about God. Let's watch and listen to what God is showing and telling us in these events."

After attending a vigil, a young woman named Andrea said, "I know what this is. Know nothing, show up, expect healing." That is the simplest and best description of the vigils. You don't need a training course before you can begin to love people. You don't need special instruction and preparation to be present in another's life. And so it all revolves around trust. Show up, know nothing. That's a lot of trust. And expect healing, most of all. Know that we have been given all that we need; we possess all that we need to heal. But all of that requires showing up.

This only makes sense if you see the vigils as an enacted prayer. A vigil is a liturgy—a carefully constructed way of being with God and with one another that is designed to elicit and express the most profound forms of dependence, trust and hope. "Know nothing, show up, expect healing" is in fact a statement of the kind of faith implicit in any act of worship—a statement that worship depends on the grace of God rather than the fitness of the participants.

The person who taught Marcia to pray was her son, Tom. He was very young and still learning speech. They were at the table, and Marcia said, "Tom, would you like to say the prayer tonight?" He said yes, so they bowed their heads. And Tom said, "Dear Lord, make my soul grow. Amen." Marcia instantly felt that it was the most beautiful prayer ever said. Because he got to the heart of life, and of God.

Live so that your soul grows. The most extraordinary thing about love, holy love, is that it's infinite. *How could I love this person more than I love him now?* You love him more! Love begets love. Love grows love. So your soul can grow. It's not like anything else in the world. What you give is the only thing you possess. How do you make your soul grow? By loving the unlovable, confronting fears, taking risks—in other words, gulping down fear so that you can love. It means saying to yourself, "Get the heck out of the way and be God's presence. Let God shine through your life." If you're fearful all the time, there's no place for that.

Prayer is the time when you self-consciously ask God to make your soul grow. And prayer is at the heart of the vigil ministry. There are a number of points of silence during the vigils. There is the wordless gathering. There is the awkwardness when the person charged with leading the vigil senses it is time for others to speak, but those others have not yet found courage or permission to find words, and the witnesses are unsure whether they should break the silence or simply wait in solidarity. There is the silence when a person has offered a word or gesture that is so profound it seems impossible to follow. And there is the silence when it seems enough has been said and the vigil is almost done, but the leader considers it best to wait to see if there is a final thought or reflection that might still surface.

These silences are not gaps between words. They are, in many ways, the heart of the vigil. They are a simple statement that if anything is going to happen in the face of loss and anger and hurt and grief and powerlessness and bewilderment and dismay, God is going to be the one to bring it about. While the vigil leader always uses words, it is seldom precisely those words that bring about transformation. The transformation comes about because those gathered discover their hand is held by a stranger who has made a commitment to share in grief and because all present realize they are being held in the palm of God's hand. It is when you know you are in the palm of God's hand that you become conscious that your soul is growing.

Young Tom's insight encourages us to take risks in faith that might enable our soul to grow. And these vigil silences are among such risks, for these are not reassuring silences. There are not soothing, familiar words from a prayer book or intimate encouragement from a habitual prayer partner or the warm, pleasant atmosphere of a crafted worship space. This is in the open air, usually in one of the city's much-avoided neighborhoods, generally around dusk and often in the face of apparent indifference or disquiet from local residents. There are invariably pieces of a puzzle that you're longing will come together and make sense. And always there is the mystery: "What was going through the minds of victim and perpetrator at this place? What is it like to die a violent death, and to see and know the person who kills you? Where do you run or drive to after taking someone's life? Do you sleep that night? Do you ever speak to another person of such a thing?"

It is in staying with such questions, such uncomfortable sensations, that the prayer of silence emerges. The silence is about staying with the nighttime until dawn comes, about staring down the horror until something beautiful appears, about naming the worst and knowing even that can be named, about staying still despite all urges to run away. It is about facing earthquake and fire together and attending to the sound of sheer silence. For in the end, silence means one thing above all: solidarity with God.

# 4

# Touch

*It is much easier to be violent than it is to be peaceful when you've developed a relationship with one and not the other, as I had. Yet I wanted change so badly. And I knew in order to achieve it I wouldn't be able to do it alone as I've done so much else in my past.*

COREY, RE-ENTRY FAITH TEAM PARTNER

*When I first encountered the coalition, I realized I was afraid to be in the presence of people who had been in prison. I had never met a former prisoner, and the thought of being with a drug dealer or murderer was frightening. I said I was not ready to be involved. But slowly I learned and accepted that God loves all of us in the same way. In God's eyes, I am no different than any other person. God calls us to love and serve one another, everyone, not simply those who are just like me.*

MIKE, RE-ENTRY FAITH TEAM MEMBER

The power of touch is an embodiment of the incarnation—in which God reaches out to touch each of our lives. Touch is an affirmation and a revelation of our earthly, contingent nature. It is the fundamental way we show one another we are not alone. When someone has been bereaved, tenderness may mean words, and it almost certainly includes some silence, but it really has to mean presence and touch—the shaking of the hand, the holding of the elbow, the pressing of the shoulder, all of which are communicating, "You are not alone in your grief." The father of the prodigal son ran and put his arms around his son and kissed him before he uttered a single word (Luke 15:20).

## TOUCHING OUR FEAR

Crucial to those in ministry is the way they learn to touch people in their fear. Mark was a partner in the re-entry ministry who had lived a really rough life. He'd been shot in the face and didn't have part of his ear and part of his jaw. It looked like someone had used a razor to slash him. Mark was forty-nine years old when he came out of prison, and he asked for a re-entry faith team to walk alongside him as he reintegrated into life outside prison.

Marcia, who was the same age as Mark, found an indescribable depth of love and understanding with Mark. She loved it when they had things that they needed to do, like going to the doctor or getting his driver's license renewed, because it meant they had time together. And they would just talk.

Mark got sick all the time, and the reason didn't occur to Marcia until she was sitting in the infectious disease clinic with him, and he was telling her how he felt. She finally said, "Darling, I think you have AIDS. I think that's why you're sick all the time. Honey, it's me, you know. I know your doctor, and he's an AIDS doctor. I think you should ask." And he said, "You won't love me." And Marcia said, "Oh, darling, I already do. You can't stop me. There's no escaping my love." But he never would come right out and admit he had contracted HIV—except by saying, "You won't love me."

Then Mark died. The night he died, he was in the hospital, and his re-entry faith team had been meeting a couple of blocks away to talk about how they could be helpful when he came home from the hospital again and what his family needed. They were all going home from their meeting when a team member got the call that Mark had died. So they all raced over to the hospital, getting there before Mark's family. When Mark's wife arrived, whom the members of the team loved very much, they were allowed to go into the room. They surrounded the bed and made a circle of hands with Mark. They all touched one another, and held Mark's hands, and prayed. The chaplain said a simple prayer, and they stood in silence.

This story shows several dimensions of what touch means in relation to ministry and in relation to fear. In the first place, Marcia had touched a person others would shun: someone who had been involved in violent crime and been incarcerated for a significant period. She had touched a person whose face had been disfigured—a person who was hard to look at. She had touched a person who had HIV, and through her touch, she had helped him recognize that the much-feared illness was one that he bore and had borne for some time. Finally, Marcia and other members of the re-entry team touched his body and through their touch realized the deeper life that God was bringing about through that death.

Touch is the way we turn looking into feeling. Touch is the way we recognize and affirm our common humanity. If Woody Allen was right that 90 percent of life is just showing up, then the silence of being present is the most important dimension of ministry. But if you are going to make the journey from observer to participant in the suffering and struggles of others— the journey from *being for* to *being with*—you need to learn how to touch.

Touch is not simply a reflex, an instinctual way to express an emotion. It is also a discipline to be learned. You must learn how to touch, when to touch and when not to touch. Sometimes it takes courage to touch someone. Marcia learned about all three aspects of the ministry of touch—and that touch is a demanding and yet vital part of ministry—from John, a man about her age who'd been in prison for over sixteen years. Marcia came to know John through a partner who had been a member of the coalition's first re-entry faith team and had later gone back to prison. While there, he'd said to John, "You've got to call my friend Marcia. Here's her number." It's hard to say no to a collect call from Durham Correctional Center, so Marcia took the call. John said, "Will you come and visit me? No one visits me." And she replied, "Of course."

John was an African American man; Marcia was a white woman. There were only a few white prisoners there. When Marcia visited John, it was difficult, even awkward, to embrace him. Yet he wanted to hug her. He wanted some tenderness. And so she hugged him.

But Marcia was conflicted. She wasn't behind glass. She came as a friend, on Sunday afternoons after church. If it was sunny and warm, they could eat outside, and she would bring lunch. But most of the time they were in a crowded cafeteria with lots of families.

Marcia kept thinking, *If John hugs me, everyone's going to think we're involved.* It was obvious to Marcia that there were already rumors about her among the other prisoners. "Who is she?" "It's John's new girlfriend." Even the prison guards seemed to look at her as if to say, "Oh, this is a romantic thing." So she would always introduce herself to the prison guards and other prisoners as the director of the Religious Coalition for a Nonviolent Durham, and she made it clear that she was married and was visiting John as a friend, to keep the story straight.

Marcia also talked it through with her husband. "Should I continue to visit John, and to give him hugs? There's so much potential for real and apparent misunderstanding here." It always came down to "What's more important—what people think about you or your faithfulness?" So she kept going, despite the risks.

Marcia considers that she could not have engaged in a friendship with John any time earlier in her life, because she wouldn't have had the maturity and the experience. She had witnessed grace in the enduring faith of those confronted with traumatic death, discovered the wellspring of trust in a marriage nurtured by forgiveness, and found her strength and purpose in humble surrender to God's indescribable love.

Marcia hugged John because that was what he needed. His family didn't call him. Nobody had been in touch with him. Prison is very lonely. So she did hug him. It seemed the right thing to do. When she didn't do it—there were times when she just thought, *I can't do this*—she felt terrible. She felt she had succumbed to the evil of the world.

So touch can be very dangerous, because it can be misrepresented and misinterpreted. But touch shows us how God loves us—gently and softly. The more you know somebody, the gentler that love is.

This story removes all sentimentality from the notion of touch. Touch is not a claim that holding hands makes everything feel better. Instead it is an acknowledgment that prison is an intensification of profound human isolation and that the way visitors relate to prisoners is subject to enormous waves of feeling. There is no doubt of John's deep need for love, for tenderness, for common humanity, for mere recognition: all of which he sought in physical touch. But equally there is no doubt that such vulnerability provides a moment for self-deception and confused desires. And this is not just a simple question of an incarcerated man starved of physical love. Marcia realized that her longing to bring succor and comfort to this man was so deep that she could be drawn into something dangerous, simply because it could have been easy to forget the difference between what John needed and what he wanted. So touch engages profound need and can let loose real danger. It is perhaps the most electric of the senses.

## TOUCHING OUR WOUNDS

Everything about being in the midst of violence tends to blend the notion of giver and receiver. Nonetheless some have lost family members to homicide and some have not. What does it feel like to be on the receiving end of this kind of ministry? Here is a brief account from Brenda, who knows what it means to have life taken from her.

> The Religious Coalition is not just a name. It's a force. It entered my life in August 2007, when my son Randolph James was murdered for "falling for a young woman in the wrong territory," as they call it. He was my youngest child at twenty-five years old at the time. I had never heard of the Religious Coalition for a Nonviolent Durham and surely didn't want to meet them at a time like that. A friend talked me into going to a meeting [a coalition monthly luncheon roundtable], and my life changed from that point on. When I walked in, I could feel the love and acceptance in that room. The people came to you and extended their welcome, friendship, ear to listen and condolences.
>
> I had never heard of a vigil, so I didn't know what to expect. The vigil was so spiritual and calming. All that wanted to take part were welcome. It gave me an outlet to say to my darling Randolph things I had no chance to say. In doing so, I felt for the first time that I turned him loose

and let him take his place with Jesus. Even though it was through many tears, my heart felt lighter than before the murder. Oh, what a gift of love that can never be repaid. When I think of the Religious Coalition for a Nonviolent Durham, I think of love, acceptance, being there in a time of need, tireless work, help for the helpless, nonjudgment. They are passionate in their quest to help those who need it. I feel God gave me a new family that was right for me, and I am so grateful.

The crucial dimension is physical presence—the smiles, shared tears, listening ears and warm human bodies that accompanied Brenda on her journey of grief. It is this kind of gentle presence that establishes bonds of acceptance and understanding, and communicates a tenderness that transcends fear and grief.

One of Sam's mottos is, "If it can't be happy, make it beautiful." His point is that there is more to life than being happy, and some of the truths discovered and friendships made and wisdom found in times of distress can be more sustaining and significant than the perpetual quest for happiness. In that sense happiness is the desire to float—perhaps even float away—while beauty is the perception of and desire for something deeper, the urge to dig, to look inside, to stay in the reality until God is disclosed. This is the power that lies in Brenda's remarkable words, quoted above: "Even though it was through many tears, my heart felt lighter than before the murder."

Beauty is found in the way the vigils encounter the paralysis of fear. On one occasion, members of the coalition and other mourners were standing on a street in the city. Abby, a minister who lived in the community, was leading a vigil for Adam, a teenager, maybe sixteen years old. His cousin had just been killed as well. Everyone could see the blood still on the pavement where Adam had perished. Marcia had canvassed the neighborhood that afternoon, inviting people. There weren't a lot of people out and around, so she had to knock on a lot of doors. It got dark early. It was winter, but it was mild. People came out of their houses, and gathered at that spot—a spot that really was *not* beautiful. It was *not* beautiful to see this young man's blood dry on the pavement. But then came the vigil. There was candlelight. Those gathered lit candles that represented God's light and God's expansive love.

For every victim, there's someone to blame, because violence is by the hand of another. There had been discord, as Marcia had gleaned from her conversations that afternoon. Some people had resisted doing the vigil for fear of further violence. Others were anxious when they learned that police officers had been invited. But as they stood there, all of them together, Marcia perceived that this was beauty. This was the fulfillment of faith. All was perfect, all was complete, all was possible, in them just being there together.

Initially Marcia had not seen the beauty—only the tragedy and the fear and the scarcity. But then, as the people came together, she realized they had all the riches in the world. They had community. They had each other. And they had an indescribable love that comes from God. The peace of Christ was there. That was beauty. It was one of the most beautiful, meaningful vigils she can remember.

Marcia later discovered she was not the only one who had felt that. She and Adam's stepfather had gone to the same high school; there were other people in his family she had met and grown to love. Whenever they see each other—and they see each other in very sad circumstances, often remembering homicide victims—there's always joy. It comes from what they shared in that moment, that fulfillment. It lingers. It was a moment that continues to radiate through this community and certainly through their respective lives.

What makes a time or a gathering beautiful? In the vigils, it is when those gathered relate to one another fearlessly—when they get out of the way and let God love them, when they allow themselves to receive that love simultaneously. People love in proportion to how they are loved. That's where the strength of people of faith lies—in that knowledge that they receive an enormous abundant love—and all the wisdom that comes with it. Beauty comes in those moments when people love fearlessly, are not afraid of what people think of them and are not afraid of the consequences.

There are two particular ways in which fearless touch is experienced in the coalition's ministry. Perhaps the most obvious is the sharing of many embraces. After almost every vigil, after all the words have been spoken and the memories shared, people spontaneously hug each other. There are few words, because there's little or nothing to say. People surrender to their sorrow and to their inability to change what is. The hug recognizes common, embodied, shared humanity. It is a way of acknowledging the precious existence of another fleshly, living body in the face of the sudden and horrifying absence of the brutally killed. Hugging becomes a need and a habit, such that complete strangers hug, ignoring conventions of race, class and gender, and instead affirming a more significant code of compassion, understanding, dignity and vulnerability.

The coalition's other experience of fearless touch is the handling of precious items connected with the homicide victim. Sometimes a photograph is brought. Sometimes a poem is found. Sometimes a picture, painted or drawn by the victim or a friend, appears as a memento of creativity and talent and unfulfilled potential. In each case, the care and tenderness with which these items are cherished is a profound contrast to the brutality and horror of their owner's moment of death. Such items are cradled much as the bread and wine are held at a communion service; somehow, through them, the great divide of death is overcome and an insight into the lasting character of the victim's place in the world is perceived. But only if they are treasured and cherished—and that is all about how they are touched. Occasionally these items are made available for others to touch. But usually they are held gently but firmly and unswervingly by family members alone and made available for viewing, but not handling, by others.

It seems that family members touch these items in the way they long to touch their deceased relative. The way they do so offers those seeking to be with them an indication of how they themselves wish to be touched. And the secret of *being with* those in such distress is to find ways of touching family members the way they touch these precious items.

## TOUCHING THE VOID

The "void" in this ministry is the perpetual anxiety, fear or realization that there's nothing you can do to make things better
after a violent death and that none of this ministry makes any
real difference. The whole point of the coalition's work is to say,
"Sure, there's nothing we can do. But we're going to *be with* you
anyway. And maybe together we'll discover something despite
the despair and paralysis of knowing there's nothing we can do."
And, so often, that is exactly what happens. But the mistake is
to forget for a moment the humility that comes from knowing
there is nothing you can do. The mistake is to forget that, for
many people who have lost loved ones, even having others present, in silence and touch, can feel insulting or threatening.

There was one particular occasion in 2005 when the void was
real and painful. It was a vigil in the most economically disadvantaged neighborhood in Durham, led by Sarah, a local Baptist minister. In the middle of the vigil, a man pulled up in a big,
expensive car. The group was standing under a tree on the clay,
on the dirt. The man got out of the car and shouted at Sarah,
"What are you doing here? This isn't your neighborhood." Every
doubt the group ever had—he touched it. Not just touched it,
stuck the knife in. It was very painful.

Sarah was grace and peace. She knew not to engage, not to
fight this, but to *allow* it, to *accept* his anger and his shouts of "get
out of my neighborhood." That was really hard. He told them he
was a Vietnam veteran. There had just been a murder in Durham
by a war veteran. So this conversation was right on the heels of
that story. When the man said, "I'm a vet," thoughts immedi-

ately flew to the violence of the war veteran.

Then he took issue with the way Sarah was interpreting Scripture. Her message illuminated God's grace and mercy in the darkness of human sorrow and dismay. She affirmed God's presence amid the violent destruction of a life by another, saying we are not being punished by God. We are all one in God. The vet said no one there understood Christianity. He said, not only were they out of bounds geographically, they were out of bounds spiritually. They were simply out of bounds.

Everyone was taken aback. Nobody left, but all were speechless. Nobody defended themselves. And so he left.

But he had been welcome. Even when he got very upset, he was still welcome. There was a simple, foundational agreement: all are welcome. And the group really meant it. This was a public vigil.

The experience taught Marcia how to touch the void—how to engage in herself and in others the fear and the anger and the cynicism and the despair that this was all a waste of time, an intrusion into grief, a well-meaning but empty gesture—in other words a parody of *being for*. She took time to come to terms with the experience and make some resolutions in the wake of it. The experience guided her to understand what defensiveness is—how viscerally and instinctively we defend ourselves. It led her to recommit herself to what it means to accept all. But she also wanted to say to him, "This *is* my neighborhood."

The whole experience led to the crucial affirmation that those who hold these vigils are not *outsiders*. This is not "outsiders coming in," even though the world would love to think of them like that. *There is no outside.* Everyone involved needs to say, "We're in it. We are *in* it. We are all in this together." It is a sign of the absence of Christ's knowledge or presence when people start thinking, "This is *my* land, this is *my* home, this is *my* money. These are *my* people—and those are *not* my people."

The most important gestures of love do not involve words. They involve presence and touch. Words can interpret, augment, amplify and clarify such gestures. But they can almost never substitute for them. If ministry gets presence and touch wrong, there is little that words can do. If ministry gets presence and touch right, words can come naturally.

# 5

# Words

*Over fifteen years I'd been arrested fourteen times. I had got out and doors were closing. I was watching my community where there was drugs and shooting everywhere. Guys had bets on me about when I'd be going back to prison. I knew that I didn't want that no more. Now I sing, "I know I've been changed, the angels in heaven done signed my name."*

TRAVIS, RE-ENTRY FAITH TEAM PARTNER

*Every year we have an annual vigil, where people are asked to stand if they have a connection, as a family member or friend, to someone who has died by homicide. I've been amazed at how many people stand up. This year, I stood up too, because I was fortunate enough to have had a friend called Tony. I'll always remember Tony, and I hear his voice often in my mind. One of the nicest things anyone has said to me was when Tony's mother, Cynthia, said, "I know Tony loved you." I loved him too.*

RON, RE-ENTRY FAITH TEAM MEMBER

*A*ll words in ministry in the wake of gun violence emerge from a relationship based on *being present in silence* and *overcoming fear through touch*. This chapter looks at the three contexts in which Christians use words: with one another, to God and for God.

## WITH ONE ANOTHER

Perhaps the biggest anxiety people have when imagining ministry to families of victims is, how do you begin the relationship in the first place? Every fear—that it is intrusion, that it is likely to provoke hostility or distress, that it is pointless, that you have no right to get involved—comes to the surface at the point of making the initial phone call. What on earth do you say?

There is often a dimension of race involved, for most often the person making the initial call to offer a vigil is Caucasian and the majority of those picking up the phone are African American or Hispanic. One thing that can happen when you have been brought up as the dominant race is that it's very easy to take over—without even thinking and with the best intentions. When you have been brought up with enormous confidence, with everything directed to you and with all the images of importance indicating that the world was built for you, it's easy to just go in and take over, because that's what you've been brought up to do, affirmed to do, told to do; you have a lot of answers and you're very confident. So the first thing is to recognize and try to set aside this impulse.

Marcia puts a great deal of thought and care into each call. The basic experience of the vigils for her has always been one of responding to immeasurable loss, to a situation that appears irredeemable. Neither she nor the person she's calling can bring the slain person back. So the call requires no less and no more than immeasurable love. God's love. Only one can help, and that is God. What Marcia thinks about before she calls is how she and the family and the perpetrator are united in God and how this mother she's about to speak to matters to her. Any clarity, any assistance, any compassion that she may offer must come from deep humility—a humility that allows her to surrender, rather than control.

When she calls, she's seeking out the mother, father, brother, sister, loved one of a homicide victim, and normally finds the mother. She introduces herself, and she says how sorry she is for their loss. And that it is her loss too. (Sometimes people, not the mothers, have said, "What are *you* sorry for? *You* didn't kill him.") After that she usually says, "I didn't meet your son, but I know that he was my brother, and he's my neighbor, and I know that Durham is very much less, is diminished by his absence. And I'm calling just to say that actually I have no words other than that. I want you to know that it's beyond any words I can say."

And the response is usually, "Yes, thank you." Marcia has a profound sense, in these calls, of falling into the arms of God, over and over and over, and being held. So the words are "I am personally very sorry. I share this loss with you as a child of God. And there are no words to describe this, but I come to offer my life, my soul, my prayers. And my faith. And to honor your child, knowing that he or she is of equal value and worth as anybody who has ever been and shall ever be."

What happens after that, almost inevitably, is that the mother receives those words and says thank you. And then, almost every time, Marcia asks, "Would you tell me about your child? I want to know." Then the mother relates the goodness and beauty and the accomplishments of her child, and that he or she did not deserve this. And, for Marcia, it is an extraordinary blessing to be able to say, "I know that your child was like mine, a gift beyond compare, a blessing, an indescribable blessing."

Then Marcia begins to speak about the vigil, saying, "We would be honored to honor your child, because he is ours. And one of the things that we feel moved to do by our faith is to bear witness to the dignity and worth of every human being. We do not earn it. It is not bestowed on us by any being or amount of money or any talent or gift. We are simply given it through the grace of God, and we possess it. It is our spiritual identity. We would like to do a vigil to honor your child, and we would love to have you there to tell us about your child and all the good memories and all the grace and goodness that was given during his lifetime. The vigils bear witness to this community that we are one—that our very selves are one in God. And they bear witness to the neighborhood where your loved one was killed. But if a vigil's not appropriate, that's fine."

Marcia has no rules on this. The only rule is to be true to the love that is present through God. But normally, the reply is, "That is wonderful," because two-thirds of the people who are killed in Durham are killed in the streets, the sidewalks or the front yards—in other words, in the open—and are seen, if not in the actual event, in the blood on the sidewalks, the crime scene, the knowledge that something really unjust has occurred. And a vigil offers an opportunity to bear witness to the goodness of the community. That's really what a vigil is—it is saying, "You are not alone. We are here for you. Your sorrow is shared, and the injustice is ours to bear with you." It bears witness to all the children and neighbors that it can be made beautiful. Within the community is enormous goodness. But it is only made real through relationship. This is the transition from *being for* to *being with*. It's no use sitting in our rooms and meditating on it. We can meditate on it and pray about it, but it is through the action of relationship that love exists.

Once the negative assumptions have been dismantled, trust can grow remarkably quickly. But when the time for the vigil comes, it is less a matter of speaking with one another and more about addressing God.

## To God

The heart of the vigils lies in the practice of lament. Lament means ceasing to try to protect God from our anger, disillusionment and despair. Lamenting means acknowledging and feeling that deep hurt and giving voice to it, toward God, in the presence of the community that holds that pain together with the one in grief. The lament psalms are powerful examples of individual people and communities shaping and voicing their pain and anger to a God who hears.

The vigils are not a time for experts or professional religious people to explain or justify why violent death occurs or to demand that actions be taken to stop such killings. They are a time for hearts publicly to open up in raw pain and to wail in sadness and grief. There's so much sorrow. There's death, injustice, alienation, retribution, estrangement, exploitation—where does it end? So there's plenty to lament about. There's nothing more powerful than to receive your own sorrow, recognizing that connection to all that is, including your brothers and sisters in this particular community and in all communities. Allowing yourself to feel such a huge level of pain and sorrow and sadness breaks your heart open. It means learning to say, "I'm allowing this pain, I'm not pushing it away. It is mine; this is as it is. This *is*. And I'm not going to move away from it. I'm going to allow it to hurt. I'm going to feel my hurt."

When Marcia reflects in solitude about a particular victim and thinks of the mother and the family, and all the goodness of that life and the gratitude to God for that life—that's when the sorrow starts, and the tears come. And once she embraces that pain, what she sees in her heart's vision is the walls of separation—what Ephesians calls the "dividing wall of hostility" (2:14 NIV). She sees those assumptions, those beliefs, those fears, those prejudices that have been implanted in her all her life. Some she moved right into, sought out all on her own; others she received just by being in and of this world. And when she lets those tears flow, she can feel that pain, and it is only then that she is able to detect those structures of division and separation—she can see them. She perceives how they have been casting shadows in her life in such a way that God's light and love can't get through.

In that state of pain and sorrow and hurt, Marcia comes to a point that there's an enormous "I surrender." She surrenders to the pain of the world, including her own. With her heart broken open, the tears seem to wash away those walls. Not all of them. But she can feel the illusion that she is separate begin to drown. She can feel the illusion of estrangement, the illusion of scarcity, drown. The tears wash those walls away, and she is filled with love, holy love. It is not experienced in her head. It is experienced in her body. She can feel her chest expanding—a strong sensation through her entire body. And she feels that she can breathe the sky and that she's simply filled. She thinks, *I am. I can see my true identity. And that true identity is a child of God.*

Marcia's path to that experience is through the pursuit or the acknowledgment or the honoring of pain. The human mind wants to flee hurt. Yet she has found that the more she goes toward death, the less fearful she becomes of it; the more she allows it to be and exist, and the more she honors it in her life and in the life of the community, the more she has energy, the more she has joy in her life, the more she understands it as an extraordinary opportunity. It's not the length of life that matters. It is in knowing that we too shall pass from this world, that we are able to live in this world in a manner that will never die. And the name of that form of existence is love. So the paradox is, the more that we attend to and honor death, the more we are of life.

Lament thus searches out the deepest places in the heart and exposes them to the presence of God. It is a whole-body experience. Part of the complexity of a vigil is that this depth of feeling is being experienced among people who do not know each other well—and sometimes not at all. And so along with the profound intimacy of hearts stretched out before God comes the profound awkwardness of not knowing what to say or how to say it.

Marcia has learned a great deal about how to act in the presence of such powerful feelings among people she does not yet know. Lament is when you cry and feel the pain of the situation, and ask for mercy, and feel the pain of your own life. And you become aware of all the times you couldn't see the truth of another person's life and could not love her or him. Something happens as you seek to love something that at first glance might not seem lovable. It's so uncomfortable that you just want it to go away. But that's not God's way. Instead you have to find a way to open your heart to that person and to *claim* him or her. You can feel your soul reaching around the person, as if she or he were in your own arms, like a baby. And this means leading with your soul, not your mind, because your mind will say, "This is awful. Get me out of here."

Marcia says to herself, *Lead with your soul—with who you really are, with the source of your life, the source of what sustains you and who you are forever.* That allows her to feel the pain and to seek that closeness and touch. Leading with her soul allows her to accept what is and not fight it and not sit in its presence, saying, "Oh, it should have been this way. Oh, I wish it was that way. Oh, how did this happen? Oh, what's going to happen next?" But just to *be with* that sorrow, and surrender to God, and know that everything we need is here and available, and not do *anything*. That's the discipline of doing nothing—doing nothing in order to allow the person and yourself to feel the pain—not to distract from it or diminish it. It is gently saying, "You don't need to be pain-free for me to love you."

While there is anger, sadness and bewilderment, the fundamental aspect of lament is grief. Lament is not a functional or utilitarian thing; nonetheless lament can be said to have reached its core when the true dimension of grief has been felt, touched, named and articulated. In that sense lament is essential to what it means to grieve well. And the less well a person has died, the more essential it is that their relatives may be afforded the support and opportunity to grieve well.

What does it mean to grieve well? Grieving well is to feel *all* the pain, because all that pain is born of love. It is easy to forget that. Marcia, like many others, grew up in a culture where people didn't show their grief—it wasn't socially acceptable. This limits the good work that grief needs to do. It doesn't mean people don't feel, but because they don't show that feeling, it becomes internalized. People get the idea that they're somehow deficient and defective if they feel pain. People of faith have done a terrible disservice to one another by thinking that, if they love God, they're not supposed to feel pain. What they sometimes need to say is, "Here I am, Lord, with all this brokenness. Shattered into a million pieces. Completely dumbfounded. Confused, angry, without power and in total pain." That is lament. And that too is a moment to trust God.

Grieving well is like this. Marcia remembers, when she was a little girl, diving into a feather bed and sinking. That's how she feels when she grieves. In that pain, she's surrounded by love.

But it's only because she shares that love that she feels the pain. To pull away and say, "Something must be wrong with me; God is not present here," is a mistake. Grieving well reveals what is not of love. That gets sorted out in the tears. Those tears wash away the walls that can be washed away and leave behind what lasts forever. That makes it possible to discern what is of love and what is not. And then you are able to address that. It's not just the deceased that you're grieving, it's fear and all these other things that need to be addressed.

There's no doubt that, in these terms, some vigils are more rewarding than others. Sometimes few if any family members are present. For example, in the case of the death of a recent immigrant, there may be no family members living in the city or even in the country. At other times there is a deafening silence, where an issue is known by key mourners but cannot be articulated for some reason, and so everything that takes place seems superficial because the truth cannot be spoken. Sometimes there is a heavy police presence, for the sake of security and safety, and significant people keep their distance. Very occasionally the person asked to lead the vigil misreads the emotions or the intensity of the situation, or the surrounding noise of traffic or other disturbances prove too distracting, and the work of the vigil is inhibited. But more often lament is expressed, and some or many present plunge into the "feather bed" of grief.

## For God

Marcia is not a pastor. She invites local clergy to lead vigils; she does not feel it is her role to lead them herself. The role of the person leading the vigil is certainly to help others speak to God and undoubtedly to help them speak with one another. But it is also, implicitly or explicitly, to speak *for* God. Difficult as this is in the face of dismay and despair, it is all the more necessary. Some truths of God must publicly be affirmed; at the same time it is good for what is unknown to be acknowledged as unknown. If the pastor affirms too much and goes beyond what can be known of God's purposes and reasons, there may be a feeling of hurt and even anger. But if the pastor affirms too little, wanting not to impose and merely to create space, the full power of the vigil is not realized.

The first question for the pastor is, "Just who do you think you are to presume you can speak in the face of horror and anger and grief?" This is how Abby, a pastor who has led several vigils, prepares:

Leading a vigil as an ordained minister creates a space of worship and prayer outside of a sanctuary. I wear my clerical collar when I lead a vigil to say that walking into circumstances of murder is holy ground. In my tradition, people associate the clerical collar with an act of worship. I am saying, "This apparently forsaken place can be as much of a place to encounter God as any building called a church. It is holy ground because it is where people have gathered in humility and expectation."

Some would say, "You have no business being there. It's not your family or your friend." When I speak as a minister with the authority of the church, I say, "This person *is* my family because they are God's family." Being ordained means saying this sometimes in ways that challenge and sometimes in ways that comfort. But it always means setting people free to live, trusting that they belong in God's family.

Anxiety about what precisely to say at a vigil is similar to the anxiety when making a first contact with a grieving family. The issue of not knowing the victim personally can be turned to the pastor's advantage, provided that the pastor concentrates on things that can be known regardless of circumstance. What is being proclaimed, after all, is unconditional acceptance— and unconditional precisely means regardless of circumstance. These are not privileges you can lose or rights you can forego— they are statements of the ultimately irresistible yet gentle love of God. Abby goes on:

> When I'm asked to lead a vigil, I choose Scripture readings that voice the tragedy and pain of the situation and at the same time evoke a sense of the healing only God can bring. Psalm 46 is one of the best: "God is our refuge and strength, a very present help in trouble. Therefore we will not fear, though the earth should change. . . . God is in the midst of the city; it shall not be moved; God will help it when the morning dawns. The Lord of hosts is with us; the God of Jacob is our refuge. . . . 'Be still, and know that I am God!'" The Scripture can allow us to hear God's own grief and at the same time draw us into the presence of God's unending love.
>
> The most important things I say for God are "God always has and always will love Kado." "Kado's life is more

than the way he died." "God holds all of his life and especially his death." "God doesn't think anyone has earned a violent death." On one occasion at a vigil, there were strikingly visible bloodstains remaining on the driveway beneath our feet, and those stains made visible the wounding of the entire neighborhood. As we stood together, I said, "God loves this ground where we stand. God created it. God will never forsake it. God loves the neighbors who have built their lives upon it. And God always will."

I have learned how significant it is to speak of the perpetrator(s). This is true whether or not there have been arrests and convictions, because often things are known about suspected perpetrators that can't be shared publicly, and these are sometimes the hardest things for a grieving family or neighborhood. Speaking of the perpetrators often happens best by remembering them in prayer, as God reminds us of the temptation to perceive and create enemies. That is best coming from God and is an essential, if challenging and sometimes uncomfortable, message of the vigils.

God comes recognizing all that is unreconciled, all that is unhealed, all the division and estrangement that become publicly visible in a violent death. God knows. God doesn't expect us to come with it all put right. God's very way of being with us propels God into the midst of all that is unreconciled between me and my brother, my sister, my neighbor.

This is perhaps one place in the coalition's ministry where it is still appropriate to speak of *working for*. The pastor has a unique role here. The vigils are about expressing feelings, but there is more to them than that. The vigils are a witness to God and to the community of grief and sorrow and anger and dismay and lament, but there is more to them even than that. The vigils are finally an expression of faith in God—a willingness to come into God's presence even—or especially—at a time of greatest distress, in hope and expectation of the three central promises of the Christian faith. There is the angel Gabriel's promise: "Emmanuel . . . God is with us" (Matthew 1:23). There is Paul's promise: Nothing can separate us from the love of God (Romans 8:38-39). And there is Jesus' promise: "Remember, I am with you always, to the end of the age" (Matthew 28:20). These are God's promises, God's promises to *be with* us always. They need to be heard and received. And this is the role of the pastor: to proclaim gently but unswervingly that however terrible these circumstances, the most important things are still true, and lie with God.

# 6

# Kingdom

*My re-entry team members and partners are my angels who protect me and care for me when I need it most. They are my angels right here on earth.*

CUBBI, RE-ENTRY FAITH TEAM PARTNER

*Since I joined the re-entry team, I have met some amazing people. I am in awe of the transformation they have made and the conviction they hold for their decision to remain straight and clean. I watch as they calmly deal with big, unusual problems that seem to occur with regular frequency. I marvel at the patience they have with society and the restrictions it places on them. I am stunned with the happiness of their lives, the fact that they dream and the hope they have for their lives.*

MIKE, RE-ENTRY FAITH TEAM MEMBER

*T*his final chapter brings together the themes of the previous five chapters by focusing on the reconciliation and re-entry ministry of the Religious Coalition for a Nonviolent Durham and, in particular, on the story of Tony—one partner who was incarcerated, was a member of a re-entry faith team and then was murdered—and on what happened next.

## RE-ENTRY

The reconciliation and re-entry ministry connects people of faith with people returning from prison and with people in the criminal justice system to restore wholeness to one another and to their community. Chapter two told the story of how Marcia realized that there was not a simple distinction between victims and perpetrators, but that everyone was in this together. This discovery was the beginning of the reconciliation and re-entry ministry. It came when Marcia realized the coalition was holding a vigil for a man she had met at a vigil six weeks earlier as he was walking past, having just been released from prison. She broke down and wept, because she realized that she had hardened her heart. She wept for all the people she had not loved. She wept for all the families she had not allowed to be authentic with her. She wept for what she saw as her terrible assumption that there were two sides. She could now see that there were no sides, that there were no enemies, that God had no enemies—and neither should she. That realization took Marcia to her knees. She could see all the ways she was separate from God. And it became very clear to her what God was calling the coalition to do. It was time to integrate ministry to perpetrators into ministry to the families of victims.

Given the countless committees that the coalition members each sat on, they began to network with others to think about changes in local policies and structures regarding perpetrators of violence, what laws they could promote, what program they could come up with, what funding they could allocate to make all the violence and guns and hatred go away. Through networking, Marcia met Gudrun, who directed the Criminal Justice Resource Center. The two women met together for about a year and talked about how they could create a ministry for perpetrators of violence in which they did no harm, in which they would be faithful to God and in which they could set about forming uncommon friendships. It's not like you can simply stand at the local prison, and say, "Hey, anybody need a re-entry team?" So they planned and prayed, and in January 2004 formed the first re-entry faith team at Epworth United Methodist Church—the church in which Marcia had grown up. Other re-entry teams were subsequently formed at local Baptist, Quaker, United Church of Christ and other churches.

Marcia met Tony through the reconciliation and re-entry ministry. Tony had come home from prison a few days before his twenty-first birthday after serving almost five years behind bars. He had heard about the re-entry faith team ministry through the Criminal Justice Resource Center, a Durham County agency that provides a range of services for people on probation or on post-release supervision, and he had requested a team as soon as he was released from prison. The team came from a local Baptist church. They promised to be present in one another's lives. And they did a great many things together. They advocated with employers where Tony applied for jobs, helped with groceries and medicine and expenses, played together, ate together, enjoyed his baby and hung out together. Together, they experienced the power of presence, of relationship, of *being with*. They also grieved for the several friends he lost to violence during the time the team knew him and joined one another in supporting the vigil ministry. At the end of every meeting, he would wrap his arms around Marcia and the other members of the team, and they would never leave one another without the gentle words, "I love you."

The kind of power such a team creates and discloses is the gift of association: no one is alone. That's the place to begin with everyone coming home from prison. There's been an illusion created in our society that we do it alone, that life is an intensely individual journey. It's not true. Success occurs in the context of relationship. The re-entry faith team is a group of people who are keeping one another accountable and are accountable not only to each other but to their church and to the Scriptures and to the tradition and to the future. They are a small picture of the church in reconciliation with the world.

One moment more than any other shows the power of association in Tony's re-entry faith team and the way their relationship of trust burst out of the huddle of mutual care and became publicly significant. It was a moment when *working with* and *working for* combined in the strength of *being with*.

Tony had been identified by the police as a person of interest. He was not absolved. All his subsequent actions were viewed under the shadow of his past offenses. He would receive citations for minor infractions. Once, at a re-entry faith team meeting, Tony said, "Well, I've got to be in court." The team was startled, and asked why. It was a minor charge: Tony had been sitting in the back of a car that was playing loud music, and everyone in the car had been cited for disrupting the peace. And the team said, "Well, we'll go. We'll just show up." So they went into the courtroom, which was a lot like a church. There were pews and a pulpit, and a choir of attorneys and court clerks. But as cases unfolded, the atmosphere was somber; there were no smiles. Tony's public defender was white. The assistant district attorney prosecuting the case was white, and the judge was white. Tony was African American. The members of Tony's re-entry team were white.

Tony's case was called. The members of the team didn't talk; they just all stood up like a silent choir behind him. A very unfriendly environment was festering. Finally the judge said, all of a sudden, "Stop. Who are *you?*" He looked at the team intently and said, "Who *are* you?" And immediately team members were saying, "We're Watts Street Baptist Church Reconciliation and Re-entry Faith Team—and he's with us. And we're here just to let you know he's this great guy and we love him dearly, and he's with us and we're with him." The district attorney and the public defender were speechless.

The judge looked down, and Marcia heard him saying, "We've been waiting for you. We've been waiting for you. This is where the church must be." And everything shifted. The feeling in that courtroom was different. People were laughing at the team's excitement, their joy of being with Tony, the love that they shared and the friendship they were expressing. The judge smiled, and his look said, "We're glad you're here."

Tony could have been skewered: every judgment, every assumption that could ever be made about a person, he was likely to find projected onto him. But after that, the attorneys cooperated. The punishment was minimal. There was an atmosphere of reconciliation. Marcia stood behind Tony and thought, *If our roles had been reversed, and I was standing there as a white person, and the judge and everybody in charge of my fate was black and didn't know where I came from—how glorious it would be if I had a black faith team sitting there saying "She's with us." What a wonderful gift that would be.*

Reconciliation and re-entry is not simply a ministry for ex-offenders. It is a ministry of reintegration of society, one relationship at a time. It assumes that offenders are the public, visible symptom and scapegoat for a society gone astray. Re-entry faith teams do for communities what twelve-step programs do for individuals: they gradually name the extent of what is wrong in the process of putting it right. They are about the reconciliation of each of us to our community and to God, and of the church to society.

Reconciliation is about personally saying, "I want to engage and be made whole with my church, with God and with my community at large." That can be done only in close proximity. It cannot be done intellectually. It requires a relationship that promises not only "I am present with you in this moment" but also "I will be present tomorrow." Marcia finds Tony is still with her, in her prayers and her imagination; and she makes decisions all the time based on her relationship with Tony.

It was not just Tony, but each member of the re-entry faith team that was transformed by their life together. Reconciliation and re-entry meant being reconciled to and re-entering relationship with God, church and community for each one of them.

## RESURRECTION

And then Tony was murdered. He was unarmed, on a road, on a late spring afternoon. Marcia got a call from Kelisha, Tony's sister, early the next morning. Marcia went straight to Tony's house after dropping off her son at school, and it immediately became clear she was being honored as a family member and so was Ron, another re-entry faith team member. Marcia gathered with some of the women of the family and prepared food.

In the subsequent hours, relationships so carefully nurtured through the years came into the story. First, a reporter came from the *Raleigh News and Observer*, but the family was naturally hesitant to talk with him. Immediately Marcia said, "It's Stan! He's a friend." All those years of talking to crime reporters about homicide and crime bore fruit in this one moment when Marcia was able to say to the family, "He's with us. He's one of us. He's in the kingdom." And Ron, a re-entry faith team member, was also the editorial page editor of the *Durham Herald-Sun*, the other local newspaper. So the family knew Tony's dignity would be affirmed in the press, and their fear was reduced.

Then came the question of the funeral. Tony and his family were members of The Wave, a growing nondenominational church based in a building too small to host the funeral. Watts Street Baptist Church, where the re-entry faith team was based, was also too small. Then Marcia asked, "What do you think about Duke Chapel?" because Tony's mother Cynthia was a longtime Duke employee. The idea seemed incredible. Duke Chapel, famous, enormous, gothic and forbidding, seemed the epitome of a church for the rich and influential. Even Marcia, who had grown up with a parent on the Duke faculty, assumed a funeral at Duke Chapel was not for the likes of her.

But the Duke Chapel community also had a re-entry faith team, including a member of the senior university administration and some members of the interdenominational Congregation at Duke Chapel, as well as Abby, the chapel's community minister, who was closely involved with the coalition. Coming from a church that didn't do anything without approval from a committee, Marcia was ready to be "committeed out." She was ready to be told, "We just can't do it, because this committee has to meet and then that committee, and that's not going to be for two weeks." Nonetheless Marcia called Abby, and Abby knew who to call. She called Sam.

To Sam, this seemed a perfect opportunity to bring together the growing community ministry of the chapel with its on-campus presence. His first encounter with the coalition (as narrated in the preface) had come when he was wondering in what kind of places Christ might show up in Durham. He was being given an offer: one of those places might be Duke Chapel.

Abby's role as community minister was to make the chapel and the more socially disadvantaged neighborhoods of Durham more visible to one another—trusting that the encounters that arose would be infused with the Holy Spirit. This encounter with Tony's family immediately looked like the most visible embodiment of that commitment. She had been forging trust and understanding by spending time in socially disadvantaged neighborhoods, taking people seriously, listening, sharing their struggles, not assuming there had to be an agenda of change—except in herself. But a sign of the fruitfulness of *being with* comes when partners find something (besides money and influence) that they have that may help others make their own journey. And the Duke Chapel sanctuary, in a time of grief and loss, was precisely such a thing.

Yet these things don't often happen. This event was going to step outside the widely assumed purpose of this glorious, neo-Gothic masterpiece, the grandest and most hallowed church building in the whole state. As Marcia said, "All these different people from all these different points of relationship said, 'What is a way to show love here?' Nobody was asking the question, 'What's the minimum we have to do?' It felt like everyone was saying, 'How can I best express love toward this family, at this time, in this community?'"

And so it was that twenty-four hours after Tony was shot, a diverse collection of people—Marcia, Abby, Sam, Tony's pastor Rodney, Rodney's wife and copastor Yolanda, and Tony's mother Cynthia—sat down in the front yard of Tony's family home to plan the funeral. Rodney was a former probation officer and had worked with the Criminal Justice Resource Center—the very organization through which the reconciliation and re-entry ministry had begun. His work as a probation officer had been his ministry, until it launched his founding of a congregation.

Rodney and Marcia discovered they shared many friends. So a whole network of relationships had woven together—from the coalition to a reporter to a local church to a university chapel to a storefront pastor—and all were connected by the re-entry ministry. These different people and institutions were re-entering one another's lives in beautiful ways. For Sam and Marcia, a friendship and shared ministry that had begun three years before had reached its most poignant moment.

The funeral turned into a three-hour vigil. There was an open microphone, and it took a long time before everyone realized that the microphone was open to all five hundred people in attendance, across race and class, across affiliation and prison time, across religious tradition and academic recognition, across verbal dexterity and emotional stability. So there was silence.

And there was plenty of touch. Tony's body lay in an open casket. He may have received more kisses from friends and family in his death than he did in his twenty-five years of life. A crowd of Cynthia's coworkers from the food halls of the university filed past the casket wearing their Duke uniforms.

And there were words. Once the silence and touch were settled, the words poured forth. Rodney preached on the prodigal son and finished with an altar call. Thirty young people, many of them gang members, came forward to declare their newfound faith, and Rodney slowly went down the line and prayed with each one of them.

The whole event took tragedy and horror, and, through the power of silence, the power of touch and the power of words, made that tragedy into a prayer. There was a power in that chapel that day that you could only call the power of God.

Of the many messages delivered at the open microphone, three stood out. One woman stepped tentatively forward and told the assembled company, "I don't know whether Tony did anything seriously wrong or not. But I do know that I was a prostitute for many years and God found a place in his kingdom for me. So I know there must be a place for Tony today."

A young Caucasian man later walked to the microphone, wearing a ragged suit and narrow tie. He looked like he had come from an office in the more alternative and bohemian side of town. He said, "I just need y'all to know that I wanted to be here for Tony and be his friend these last couple of years, because he was my only friend during the loneliest years of my life. And that was when he had the cell next door to me." Suddenly it was obvious that they had been in prison together—and formidable stereotypes about race were questioned for a moment, and it was clear that if this man had such a story to tell, anyone present could have been in the cell next door to Tony.

Later, a man of enormous stature in Durham's culture of violence came up and said, with undeniable eyes and fixed conviction, "No retribution. If we're going to honor Tony, we will not shoot each other. We're not going to do violence in his name." And suddenly it became apparent that people's lives were at stake in the way Tony's life was being honored.

The day ended with a reception in the dining hall where Cynthia worked, which the university had offered to the family. Marcia remembered that this was the same dining hall where she had eaten as a freshman at Duke, thirty years before. For her, this was the final reintegration on a day of so many.

This was a death. But it was also a resurrection. Why describe it as resurrection? Marcia's overwhelming sensation in the whole sequence of events was a feeling that began, but did not end, with a sense of failure. The re-entry ministry had been born at a vigil, when Marcia recognized the presence of a young man who had just come home from prison. But Tony was not just a young man who had come out of prison. He was a re-entry partner—and the re-entry ministry was designed for people just like him. Tony's re-entry faith team members had walked with him to help him avoid the violence that had checkered his life. And although Tony had lived a different life after incarceration, he had still died violently.

The immediate reaction was to avoid naming that, because his death felt like a failure to the re-entry faith team and to the whole re-entry ministry. But the lesson Marcia learned in her grief was that the length of a life has no relationship to the impact of a life. With faith, time becomes something else. Time is reckoned against eternity. In the light of resurrection, life is measured on a different scale—by the quality of its light, grace, goodness and love—not by its length.

Much of the world evaluates success in terms of measurable results. But a life of relationship—when you're living and looking through the eyes of God—shatters that idea of success and failure. Marcia pleaded with God to explain this to her and to forgive her for failing to protect Tony. She felt her heart break open, and she had an enormous, tangible experience of feeling her capacity to love grow. She felt she was in the presence of Tony.

After Marcia had this experience of *being with* Tony beyond death, her prayers changed. Every time she prays, whether it's in the middle of the night or throughout the day, she is always thanking God for all the souls who came before her and all the souls who will come after her. This has become a gift. She feels Tony *with* her, all the time. From this very sad, tragic incident—murder—Marcia's faith grew, and her life changed, but for the better. It taught her *never* again to move away from the tragedy and the suffering of the community. And it is hard for her to believe that change could have happened without her experience of loss and suffering.

This is fittingly called resurrection because it takes not just the *power* of sin and death but also the *effects* of sin and death in the poisoning of relationships and communities and in the withering of the social imagination, and transforms them into means of grace and forms of abundant life. This is exactly what resurrection does. Resurrection means bringing life out of death—not just leaving the shell of death behind, but watching as the sites and locations of death are transformed—gradually or suddenly—into the places of abundant life. Tony's funeral was an occasion when life came out of death. It wasn't happy, but it was beautiful.

In a story of many harmonies and many agonies, there was, for Marcia, one profound irony. Tony was her friend—such a close friend that she was almost absorbed into his family. In more than 150 vigils, she had never been so involved with the family of a victim. And so, when it came to holding a vigil for Tony, for the first time Marcia was genuinely on the receiving end of the co-alition's ministry; it was the first time she had ever been to the vigil as part of the family receiving the love of the community. For the first time she had the opportunity to stand and publicly say to strangers, "Tony was a great man and friend, whom I will love forever."

Being in the warmth of his family, being aligned with his friends, made her soul grow. This was not another invisible inci-dent that people were going to look away from in judgment and horror. People could not say, "This is not *us*, it has nothing to do with *us*, it is not in *our* neighborhood, we didn't know the per-son, there's nothing we can do." Instead, all these people came forward and said, "I bear witness to your pain." And in doing that, they unburdened Marcia. They carried her pain.

What Marcia discovered when tragedy came to her own door was that we don't have to make it come out with a good ending in order for it to be about the kingdom of God. We have to put ourselves in a place where the kingdom will break in upon us and then simply be there for it. That's what happened in this situation. Marcia *surrendered* to God and was held up by an enor-mous holy love.

This had been one of the most tragic things that had ever hap-pened to her, and the response was an unbelievable gracious-ness. The response was not, "What is the minimal amount I can do, how can I get out of it, how can I separate myself, how am

I not a part of that?" Instead, everyone said, "I *am* a part of that, and I *will* be a part of this." The enormous love was transformational for Marcia. And it was transformational for the thirty people who came forward during Tony's funeral to the front of the chapel, who recognized that their hurt could be transformed in their response to this tragedy, instead of going back to their associations and arming and retaliating. Together they said, "We are one another's keepers. More than anything we could ever imagine, we *are* one another's."

Marcia's ministry had turned right around. She had become the needy one who had the feelings of loss and bewilderment in the face of her friend's sudden, violent death. But now she was surrounded by all those from whom she had not separated herself in their moment of grief and isolation. She was reaping the harvest of her silent presence, her gentle touch and her timely words.

RECONCILIATION

It is time to reiterate what this particular ministry has disclosed about God.

God's fundamental mode of being is *being with* us. This is what we learn at every stage of Jesus' story. In coming among us in the incarnation, God in Christ "hung out" with us. In doing so, God demonstrated a profound enjoyment of us. God has no purpose for us beyond a longing to *be with* us and enjoy us forever. In abiding with us in Nazareth, God showed us an identity in Christ that is shaped not primarily to achieve tangible results but to forge inexhaustible relationships. In journeying with us around

Galilee, God manifested in Christ a commitment to *be with* us in our griefs, our sicknesses, our waywardness, our fears and our misunderstandings. In hanging for hours on the cross and not coming down as the bystanders and authorities goaded him to do, God showed us in Christ a love that abides, that perseveres, that remains present to us, however bad things are, for however long it takes; a love that sticks around, a love that stays put, a love that hangs on. That's what the cross is: a love that hangs on. In the resurrection, God made clear to us in Christ that nothing—neither death nor life—can separate us from God's love. And in the sending of the Spirit, God promised to *be with* us always, to the end of time, and to empower us to be Christ for others and find Christ in them, beyond our own strength and courage.

The story this book has told is of how Marcia's attempts to find a way of responding to a social crisis in her hometown were a journey toward coming face to face with this God. Her original attempts were shaped by a different notion of God. Her desire to solve the situation through legislation and policy and lobbying presupposed a God who "solves" our problems without truly *meeting* us—without the reality of the incarnation, without the cost of the crucifixion. Even her early endeavors to hold vigils and meet victims' loved ones were still captivated by the word *for* rather than the word *with*.

But Marcia's conversion took place when she realized she was arranging a vigil for a man who had himself been present at a vigil not long before. Her hardened heart melted, and she realized that the whole ministry was about *with* rather than *for*. The whole ministry was about breaking down the dividing wall of *us* and *them*. The whole ministry was about discovering that God has no enemies. The whole ministry was about the abundance of God's boundless love in the face of the scarcity of our fear, our prejudice and our avoidance of death. When Marcia found out what made her soul grow, she realized the places and the people who truly were the presence of God. Avoiding those places, those feelings, those realities, turned out to have been avoiding God.

The poignancy of the vigils is that they highlight—and "walk toward"—the *absence* of the victim. They do not try to abolish that absence with policy, strategy or expertise, or rectify it with judgment or punishment. Instead they face that absence with a different kind of presence—the presence of companions who can't make things better, can't make things happy, but can point to and exhibit a number of qualities of solidarity that are summed up in the word *with*.

The social crisis of a high level of gun violence is, more than anything else, a personal and relational crisis of *not-being*—of coping with the sudden and violent death and absence of a living, loving human being. The philosophical witness of the coalition's ministry is the determination to make up for in the word *with* what is, in the desperate moments of grief, so painfully missing in the word *being*.

*Being with* is fundamentally an attempt to imitate God, because it is precisely what God does in the face of our deaths— our own non-being. God is *with* us. God is the being who is fundamentally, definitively, ultimately *with*. Abundantly, sufficiently, stubbornly, relentlessly. And so our response is simply stated. We are to *be with* God. *Being with* one another is the way we imitate and proclaim and witness to the way God is *with* us. Everything about God is communicated in that word *with*. And so everything about the coalition seeks to be channeled through that same word, *with*. The coalition is nothing less than a bold theological proclamation about the very nature of God, made known in the face of death.

Marcia began by trying to bring about peace without requiring reconciliation. That was what the technology of legislation offered: making a better world without us needing to become better people. She failed. She then set about a long journey of helping people be reconciled with one another. In the process she realized that we cannot fundamentally be reconciled with one another unless we are reconciled with God. But only when she herself was a victim's loved one, only when she was the one weeping and helpless when the blood of a man she loved was crying out from the ground, did she come to a place where she had to be reconciled with God. It was no longer a process she facilitated for others: it was a ministry she desperately needed for herself.

That was when she finally realized what reconciliation truly means: discovering that God dwells precisely in these moments, and that Christ's suffering presence is not God's answer, not God's solution, but God's love. And that meeting God and finding yourself lie in eternally enjoying and embodying that present, suffering love.

# Ten Gleanings

*H*ere are ten gleanings derived from the teachings of loved ones of homicide victims, former prisoners, re-entry faith team members, coalition friends and many prayers. Each lesson Marcia has learned through the practice of presence has been revealed as a paradox: birth in death, possession through giving, wisdom disclosed by the unknowable.

1. The only judgment I will make of others is that we are equally blessed by God.

2. I discover the joy of my particularity in the context of God's infinite abundance.

3. I am living in eternity. I measure success by the expression of God's presence, not by prescribed outcomes.

4. The most important question to ask myself before addressing difficulty or conflict is, "Do I accept and love this person as I am accepted and loved by God?"

5. My fears subside when I remember my soul—my existence in the heart of God.

6. My soul is for all, because my soul is with all. We are all one in God.

7. The joy of love lives among suffering, including my own.

8. Receiving God's love is like breathing in. Responding to the suffering of others is like breathing out. If I do the first without doing the second, I will pass out.

9. Healing is God's greatest mystery. I can't explain it. I can't avoid it.

10. The heart of justice is mercy. Justice begins when I stop judging.

# Study Guide

*Questions for Personal Reflection or Group Discussion*

## Introduction and Chapter 1: Nazareth

1. What social issue or problem in your community breaks your heart? What needs are you passionate about, and how do you try to address them?

2. Sam and Marcia present four ways of engaging others—*working for, working with, being for* and *being with*. Which way of engagement is natural for you? Is there one that you would like to work toward practicing more?

3. Can you think of a situation that seems to demand *working for*? What kind of relationships develop in that situation? What are the limits of those relationships?

4. Think of an example when Jesus practices being with or being for in the Gospels. What can we learn from his example about how to inhabit these forms of engagement well?

## Chapter 2: Ministry

1. What ministries do you or your church participate in regularly? How were you called to those ministries?

2. In your own experience of ministry, what kinds of engagement have drawn you closer to Jesus and his kingdom? Have
you had experiences that left you frustrated? Have you
walked away from any ministries because of frustration or
disappointment?

3. What did Marcia learn in the process of coming to "be for"
victims of gun violence? How might *being for* change the way
you do ministry in your own context?

4. Sam writes that Marcia "found a humility that overcomes
fear and replaces it with love." What conviction makes this
kind of humility possible? What practices embody this kind
of humility?

5. How did *being for* affect Marcia's understanding of *working for*?
How do these different modes of engagement depend on one
another?

6. What moved the Coalition from *working for* to *working with*?
How might this shift in engagement change the ministry you
are part of?

## Chapter 3: Silence

1. What is the difference between being *silenced* and choos-
ing to be *silent*? What role does vigil play in a ministry of
presence?

2. The silent prayer of early Christian monasticism included a
commitment "not to flee" from demons and evil thoughts.

How has the Coalition embodied this commitment in their ministry? What has emerged from their stability in the face of violence?

3. How much time have you spent listening in your place of ministry? What do you hear when you do listen?

4. "Prayer is the time when you self-consciously ask God to make your soul grow," Sam and Marcia write. What makes your soul grow? Are there obstacles that keep your time with others in ministry from turning into a time of prayer?

5. How is silence "solidarity with God"? What does that mean for you in your life?

## Chapter 4: Touch

1. Think of a painful time in your life when you were touched. Was it a comforting touch? a violating touch? Why is touch so powerful— for good and for ill—even when it is gentle?

2. What does it mean to say that touch is a discipline? How do we learn to touch well?

3. Are there people or places in your life that you are afraid to touch? How does this fear affect your ministry?

4. What are Sam and Marcia referring to when they write about "touching the void"? Can you think of a time when you've touched the void in your own ministry? How do you pray in that place?

## Chapter 5: Words

1. Can you think of a time in ministry when you have stuck your foot in your mouth? How do you know when you have said the wrong thing?

2. What has Marcia learned about how to talk to people who are victims of violence? What kind of words help us to connect with people who are not like us?

3. Where did you learn how to talk to God?

4. What concrete practices facilitate the practice of lament for Marcia? How have you learned to lament?

5. Why do we dare to speak for God? What are the dangers? What are the gifts of proclamation to the community? To us?

## Chapter 6: Kingdom

1. Think of the most difficult time in your own life that you can remember. Who did you turn to? How was that person/group a faith team to you?

2. What did Tony's faith team offer him? What did Tony give to them?

3. What signs of resurrection do you see in the story of the Coalition's relationship with Tony? Can you name when the seeds of these signs were sown?

4. How do we measure the success of the ministries we are in-

volved in? What end are we working toward? What signs of progress should we look for?

5. What is the theological significance of the story told in this chapter? What does it teach us about who God is?

6. Read the "10 Gleanings" after this chapter. Which is most poignant to you right now? What gleaning are you taking away from this book?

# Notes

## Chapter 1: Nazareth

[1]Reconciliation and re-entry teams are a key part of the ministry of the Religious Coalition for a Nonviolent Durham. Teams consist of a re-entry partner (a man or woman who has just been released from prison) and about six members, each of whom is involved in a local congregation. This ministry is described in chapter six.

[2]The Brady Campaign to Prevent Gun Violence, "Facts on Gun Violence," <www.bradycampaign.org/facts/gunviolence?s=1>; Children's Defense Fund, "Protect Children Not Guns 2009," <www.childrensdefense.org/child-research-data-publications/data/protect-children-not-guns-report-2009.pdf>; Illinois Council Against Gun Violence, "Facts," <www.ichv.org/facts-about-gun-violence/>; and the National Education Association Health Information Network, "Statistics: Gun Violence in Our Communities," <www.neahin.org/programs/schoolsafety/gunsafety/statistics.htm>.

[3]The categories *working for*, *working with* and *being with* are adapted from Sarah White and Romy Tiongco, *Doing Theology and Development: Meeting the Challenge of Poverty* (Edinburgh: Saint Andrew Press, 1997), pp. 11-15. Neither author has developed these ideas further. The notion of *being for* is described in David Kelsey, *Eccentric Existence: A Theological Anthropology*, 2 vols. (Louisville, Ky.: Westminster John Knox, 2009), pp. 803-7.

[4]These words echo the self-description offered by Tom Cornell, "A Brief Introduction to the Catholic Worker Movement," <www.catholicworker.org/historytext.cfm?Number=4>.

[5]See White and Tiongco, *Doing Theology and Development*, p. 14.

[6]And it shifts from people being the objects of ministry to becoming partners and colaborers in ministry. This is why the Religious Coalition gives the name *partner* to the members of its re-entry teams who have recently been released from prison.

[7]This paragraph is a paraphrase of White and Tiongco, *Doing Theology and Development*, p. 14.

[8]Irenaeus of Lyons, *Against the Heresies* 4.20.7. "For the glory of God is a living man; and the life of man consists in beholding God. For if the manifestation of God which is made by means of the creation, affords life to all living in the earth, much more does that revelation of the Father which comes through the Word, give life to those who see God." Available at <www.ccel.org/ccel/schaff/anf01.ix.vi.xxi.html>.

[9]Augustine, *On Christian Doctrine*, trans. J. F. Shaw (Edinburgh: T & T Clark, 1892), bk. 1, chaps. 3-4, p. 9.

# About the Duke Divinity School Center for Reconciliation

## OUR MANDATE

Established in 2005, the center's mission flows from the apostle Paul's affirmation in 2 Corinthians 5 that "God was in Christ reconciling the world to himself" and that "the message of reconciliation has been entrusted to us."

In many ways and for many reasons, the Christian community has not taken up this challenge. In conflicts and divisions ranging from brokenness in families, abandoned neighborhoods, urban violence and ethnic division in the United States to genocide in Rwanda and Sudan, the church typically has mirrored society rather than offering a witness to it. In response, the center seeks to form and strengthen transformative Christian leadership for reconciliation.

## OUR MISSION

Rooted in a Christian vision of God's mission, the Center for Reconciliation advances God's mission of reconciliation in a divided world by cultivating new leaders, communicating wisdom and hope, and connecting in outreach to strengthen leadership.

## OUR PROGRAMS

- Serving U.S. and global Christian leaders through an annual five-day Summer Institute and other gatherings and workshops
- African Great Lakes Initiative serving leaders in Uganda, southern Sudan, eastern Congo, Rwanda, Burundi and Kenya
- Annual Reconcilers' Weekend featuring leading practitioners and theologians
- In-depth formation in the ministry of reconciliation through residential programs at Duke Divinity School
- Teaching Communities apprenticeships in exemplary communities of practice
- Resources for Reconciliation book series
- Visiting Practitioner Fellows
- Pilgrimages of pain and hope for students and others in the U.S. and Africa

## HOW YOU CAN PARTICIPATE

- *Pray for us and our work.*
- *Partner financially with the center.*
- *Join the journey.* Whether you are a student, pastor, practitioner, ministry leader or layperson, the center wants to support you in the journey of reconciliation. Explore our website and see how we might connect. <http://divinity.duke.edu/initiatives-centers/center -reconciliation>

*Please contact us for more information about the program or to help support our work.*

The Center for Reconciliation
Duke Divinity School
Box 90967
Durham, NC 27708
Phone: 919.660.3578
Email: reconciliation@div.duke.edu
Website: <http://divinity.duke.edu/initiatives-centers/
center-reconciliation>

**ABOUT RESOURCES FOR RECONCILIATION**

Resources for Reconciliation pair leading theologians with on-the-ground practitioners to produce fresh literature to energize and sustain Christian life and mission in a broken and divided world. This series of brief books works in the intersection between theology and practice to help professionals, leaders and everyday Christians live as ambassadors of reconciliation.

**Reconciling All Things**
*A Christian Vision for Justice,*
*Peace and Healing*
Emmanuel Katongole and Chris Rice

**Living Gently in a Violent World**
*The Prophetic Witness of Weakness*
Stanley Hauerwas and Jean Vanier

**Welcoming Justice**
*God's Movement Toward Beloved Community*
Charles Marsh and John M. Perkins

**Friendship at the Margins**
*Discovering Mutuality in Service and Mission*
Christopher L. Heuertz
and Christine D. Pohl

**Forgiving As We've Been Forgiven**
*Community Practices for Making Peace*
L. Gregory Jones and Célestin Musekura

**Living Without Enemies**
*Being Present in the Midst of Violence*
Samuel Wells and Marcia A. Owen